Trail Guide

EIGHTEENTH EDITION

*The Official Guide to Traveling
the C&O Canal Towpath and
Great Allegheny Passage,
from Washington, D.C. to Pittsburgh*

**GREAT
ALLEGHENY
PASSAGE**
CONSERVANCY

ACKNOWLEDGEMENTS

This publication was originally envisioned and brought to life by Linda McKenna Boxx, longtime president of the Allegheny Trail Alliance, whose love for the Great Allegheny Passage and C&O Canal Towpath is reflected in TrailGuide's narrative and selection of artwork, maps, and photos. The work of Linda McKenna Boxx in developing the narrative of this book is greatly appreciated and used with permission.

Additionally, our thanks go to Karen Gray, Ph.D., for National Park Service photos and information, to Thomas F. Hahn's and his nicely revised *Towpath Guide to the C&O Canal*, to Mike High and his *C&O Canal Companion*, to Mary Shaw and Roy Weil for their inspirational *Linking Up*, and a variety of interviews, web sources and articles. We appreciate photographers Steve Dean, Paul g Wiegman, John Urman, we are the Richards, Allegany Media, and many others individually credited who graciously allowed us to use their pictures. We thank Jim Taggart for his map work and Paul McGehee for his lovely art. Graphic design by the talented and patient Jon Miller makes *TrailGuide* stand out.

If you have pictures to share that capture the beauty of the Great Allegheny Passage or C&O Canal Towpath, please email us at admin@gaptrail.org.

Funding in part was provided by the Somerset, Fayette, and Westmoreland Counties' Tourism Grant Programs. Information is presented as a service and is not intended as a review or a recommendation.

Published by the Great Allegheny Passage Conservancy
P. O. Box 228, Homestead, PA 15120
www.gaptrail.org

Graphic Designer: Jon MIller
Cover Photo: Kelsey Ripper
Background Photo: Doug Schwab

Printed by Reed and Witting, Pittsburgh, Pennsylvania

TABLE OF CONTENTS

THE RIDE OF YOUR LIFE

From the tidewater of the Potomac River to the forks of the Ohio River – the 184.5-mile Chesapeake & Ohio Canal Towpath and the 148.8-mile Great Allegheny Passage join to form an unparalleled biking and hiking adventure.

This world-class journey, 333.3 miles long, connects Washington, D.C. to Pittsburgh, Pennsylvania, connecting in Cumberland, Maryland, to form what *National Geographic Adventurer* calls "an American classic." Every year, thousands of cyclists and hikers take this journey of a lifetime; each trip unique, exciting and full of adventures.

Starting in Washington D.C.'s Georgetown neighborhood, the C&O Canal Towpath runs adjacent to the canal's magnificent stone aqueducts, earthen dams, and hand-built lock structures which once relied on the properties of water, gravitational forces, and human ingenuity to provide a navigable route to Cumberland alongside the treacherous Potomac River.

Winding in and out of hamlets that grew out of the canal economy, and providing access to nearby towns in West Virginia (Harpers Ferry and Shepherdstown) and Maryland (Brunswick, Sharpsburg, Williamsport, Hancock, Little Orleans, and Cumberland), the towpath is known for its quiet, forested character, and dozens of campgrounds, lock houses, interpretive sites, and visitor's centers. Travelers pass by Great Falls Tavern and Overlook, near Fort Frederick, within a stone's throw of Harpers Ferry National Historical Park, across the Appalachian Trail, and through the Paw Paw Tunnel.

While the towpath is managed by the National Park Service as part of the C&O Canal National Historical Park, it is also supported by volunteers organized by the C&O Canal Trust and C&O Canal Association.

At Cumberland, the towpath joins abandoned rail lines now transformed into the Great Allegheny Passage, which meanders through four tunnels and across 12 impressive bridges constructed to tame the rugged Allegheny Mountains. From its first section within Ohiopyle State Park developed in 1978 to its final mile through Pittsburgh's steel valley in 2013, the GAP is a testimony to brilliant engineering and backbreaking physical labor – much of it by local volunteer groups – to create and maintain a smooth and nearly level path through some of the most spectacular scenery in the eastern United States.

The GAP is known for its hospitable trail towns (Cumberland, Frostburg, Meyersdale, Rockwood, Confluence, Ohiopyle, Connellsville, West Newton, McKeesport, Homestead, and Pittsburgh's South Side) and their biker-friendly, hiker-friendly cafes, inns, guesthouses, restaurants, and outfitters. It's also known for fishing, paddling, and birdwatching along the Casselman, Youghiogheny, and Monongahela Rivers, and for side trips on foot (the Laurel Highlands Hiking Trail or Ferncliff Peninsula) or by shuttle (Fallingwater or Flight 93).

Together, these paths provide a rich journey marking the opening of the "original American west," one with great views, hospitable stops, and the making of a perfect adventure.

Day riders at the Eastern Continental Divide along the Great Allegheny Passage.

Photo: Doug Riegner

MILEAGE AND ELEVATION

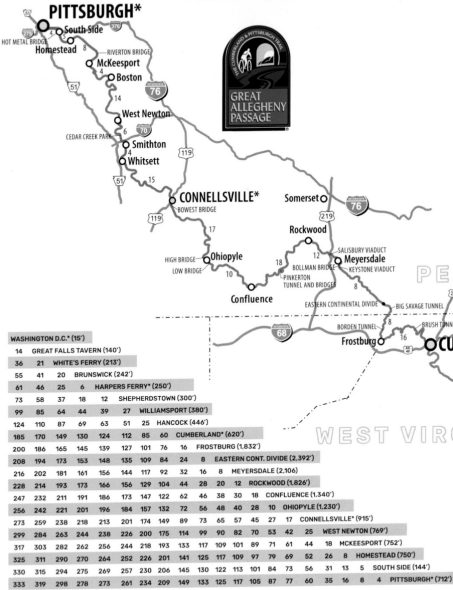

THE CUMBERLAND & PITTSBURGH TRAIL

GREAT ALLEGHENY PASSAGE

																				Location
																				WASHINGTON D.C.* (15')
14																				GREAT FALLS TAVERN (140')
36	21																			WHITE'S FERRY (213')
55	41	20																		BRUNSWICK (242')
61	46	25	6																	HARPERS FERRY* (250')
73	58	37	18	12																SHEPHERDSTOWN (300')
99	85	64	44	39	27															WILLIAMSPORT (380')
124	110	87	69	63	51	25														HANCOCK (446')
185	170	149	130	124	112	85	60													CUMBERLAND* (620')
200	186	165	145	139	127	101	76	16												FROSTBURG (1,832')
208	194	173	153	148	135	109	84	24	8											EASTERN CONT. DIVIDE (2,392')
216	202	181	161	156	144	117	92	32	16	8										MEYERSDALE (2,106')
228	214	193	173	166	156	129	104	44	28	20	12									ROCKWOOD (1,826')
247	232	211	191	186	173	147	122	62	46	38	30	18								CONFLUENCE (1,340')
256	242	221	201	196	184	157	132	72	56	48	40	28	10							OHIOPYLE (1,230')
273	259	238	218	213	201	174	149	89	73	65	57	45	27	17						CONNELLSVILLE* (915')
299	284	263	244	238	226	200	175	114	99	90	82	70	53	42	25					WEST NEWTON (769')
317	303	282	262	256	244	218	193	133	117	109	101	89	71	61	44	18				MCKEESPORT (752')
325	311	290	270	264	252	226	201	141	125	117	109	97	79	69	52	26	8			HOMESTEAD (750')
330	315	294	275	269	257	230	206	145	130	122	113	101	84	73	56	31	13	5		SOUTH SIDE (144')
333	319	298	278	273	261	234	209	149	133	125	117	105	87	77	60	35	16	8	4	PITTSBURGH* (712')

Distances are rounded to the nearest mile; an asterisk (*) denotes locations with Amtrak's Capitol Limited service.

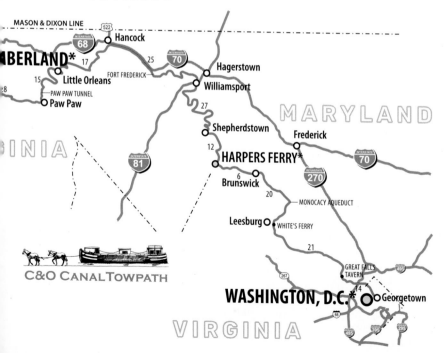

C&O CANAL TOWPATH

A PASSAGE WEST

> *Extend the inland navigation of the Eastern waters, communicate them as near as possible with those which run the westward. Open these to the Ohio, and such others as extend from the Ohio towards Lake Erie.*
>
> —Letter from George Washington, 1784

Early British colonists, from Captain John Smith to George Washington, explored the eastern seaboard looking for trade routes and passages west, past the barrier of the Appalachian Mountains and into the Ohio River valley.

"Old C & O Canal at Georgetown"

© Paul McGehee
paulmcgeheeart.com

The Potomac River was a promising route and the new nation's capital would sit at its fall line. There the broad tidewater Potomac, navigable by ships to and from the Atlantic Ocean, changed to an upland river valley that penetrated deep into the mountains in the center of the newly formed states.

Veterinary hospital at Lock 3, circa 1900.

Courtesy of the National Park Service, Chesapeake and Ohio Canal NHP.

Long before the invention of the railroad, canals were the best means of transporting goods over long inland distances, with mule-drawn boats passing through a series of lift locks. Young George Washington, on behalf of family and investors, promoted the idea of building skirting canals around falls and rapids to make the Potomac River more navigable. These early endeavors inspired the creation of the Chesapeake and Ohio Canal, with the Forks of the Ohio – present-day Pittsburgh – as the goal.

George Washington's Potowmack Company began construction in 1785 on a series of short canals to bypass the series of waterfalls upriver from Georgetown on the south side of the river. This early canal was replaced by the more ambitious Chesapeake and Ohio Canal, championed by Charles Fenton Mercer. The C&O Canal broke ground on July 4, 1828, the same day the cornerstone was being laid for the Baltimore & Ohio Railroad in Baltimore. The new technology of railroads was just emerging and the B&O was a bold venture for an unproven transportation newcomer.

BUILDING THE C&O CANAL TOWPATH

A Sunday outing, Paw Paw Tunnel, East Portal.

Courtesy of the National Park Service, Chesapeake and Ohio Canal NHP.

Canal laborers dug out the ditch that paralleled the Potomac River with picks, shovels and gunpowder. Historians estimate that about 35,000 laborers, mostly European immigrants, were employed to build the canal and all its 1,300 structures.

When finished 22 years later, the waterway averaged 50 feet wide and six feet deep, and was 184 miles long. It included 11 hand-hewn stone aqueducts and the remarkable 3,118-foot long brick-lined Paw Paw tunnel. Seven dams were used to feed water from the Potomac River into the canal ditch. Hundreds of culverts were built to divert smaller streams and excess water under the canal. Seventy-four lift locks adjusted the water levels for the 605-foot difference in elevation between tidewater in the east and its western terminus in Cumberland, Maryland.

Sections opened for navigation as they were completed: Georgetown to Seneca in 1831; then to Harpers Ferry in 1833; to near Hancock in 1839; and its ultimate terminus in Cumberland in 1850, eight years after the B&O Railroad had arrived and continued heading west. In 1852 railroad reached the Ohio River at Wheeling, West Virginia (then in Virginia); the canal never did. Only 184 miles of George Washington's grand vision was completed, leaving the task of crossing the mountains to the railroads.

For nearly a century the Chesapeake and Ohio Canal was the lifeline for communities and businesses along its route as it floated huge amounts of coal, lumber, grain, and other products to market, including essential coal and farm produce to sustain the District of Columbia during the Civil War.

Canal barges waiting to unload in Georgetown, circa 1905.

Courtesy of the National Park Service, Chesapeake and Ohio Canal NHP.

DECLINE OF CANAL TRAVEL

From the start, the C&O Canal was competing with a powerful new rail-based form of transportation. Handicapped by dry spells, floods, and winter freezes, the canal could not match the speed and dependability of the railroads. Loss of business to its rival and costly flood damage combined to close the canal in 1924. By this time, it was controlled by the B&O, which had purchased its repair bonds to prevent competitors from acquiring the corridor. The courts allowed the canal to cease operations, since the Western Maryland Railway was now open and precluded the B&O from having a monopoly.

But then the tables turned on the B&O. In 1938 after the Great Depression, the railroad received a loan from the federal government and used the assets of the C&O Canal as collateral. Later that year, the loan negotiations were concluded and the canal became the property of the federal government as part of the settlement.

The canal shared the narrow corridor along the Potomac River, east of Harpers Ferry, circa 1909.

Courtesy of the National Park Service, Chesapeake and Ohio Canal NHP.

For a quarter of a century, the fate of the canal property was fiercely debated. Some wanted to see the towpath paved into a scenic highway, others wanted to dam the Potomac for power generation, thereby flooding much of the canal, while still others wanted its natural beauty protected.

In 1954, Justice William Douglas led a contingent during a hike to preserve the canal.

Photo courtesy of George Washington University, Department of Special Collections, Gelman Library.

THE DOUGLAS HIKE

In early 1954 an editorial page exchange between Supreme Court Justice William Douglas and the editors of the *Washington Post* led to a famous eight-day hike beginning on March 20 along the towpath. Widely covered by the media, this event brought critical national attention to the preservation of the canal.

After nearly twenty more years of bureaucratic and congressional wrangling, President Richard Nixon signed a bill creating the C&O Canal National Historical Park on January 8, 1971, protecting the corridor and its structures.

THE CANAL AND TOWPATH TODAY

Many artifacts of this amazing, non-motorized transportation system can be seen today, protected and interpreted by the National Park Service. The locks were operated by lock tenders and their families. Many lock tenders' houses remain standing today, in various stages of repair. Some have been restored and are available for overnight stays through the C&O Canal Trust. (www.canalquarters.org)

Along the towpath are hundreds of structures to explore, built to create the workings of the canal system. Paw Paw Tunnel, between Mile 155.2 and 155.8, was the most difficult structure to build. It contributed to the delay in reaching Cumberland, and ultimately bankrupted the contractor. Passing through the tunnel today is a memorable part of any thru-trip.

The eleven stone aqueducts built to carry the canal over intersecting rivers that flow into the Potomac are special features to be explored as you pass by. They are elegant, arched structures built by hand from rock from nearby quarries. The lower five aqueducts are multiple-arched, while the upper six are single-arched.

C&O Canal Stone Aqueducts	
Mile	
22.8	Seneca
42.2	Monocacy
51.5	Catoctin
69.4	Antietam
99.6	Conococheague
116.1	Licking Creek
123.0	Tonoloway
136.6	Sideling Hill Creek
140.9	Fifteenmile Creek
162.4	Town Creek
180.7	Evitts Creek

The elegant seven-arch Monocacy Aqueduct was restored in 2005.

Photo: Steve Dean

Several NPS visitor centers are located along the canal. Great Falls and Cumberland visitor centers operate year-round, while the others have limited seasonal schedules. Stop in for trip planning information, to see the exhibits, or browse in the gift shop.

RISE AND FALL OF THE RAILROADS

Western Maryland Railway engine chugs through Big Savage Tunnel.

Photo courtesy of William Price Collection, Lewis J. Ort Library, Frostburg State University.

The first long distance railroad in the United States was the pioneering Baltimore & Ohio Railroad (B&O), which broke ground in 1828. Organized by business interests in Baltimore, the B&O challenged the canals in the race to reach the Ohio River. It was a daring undertaking at a time when there were only three other railroads in the country – none more than a dozen miles long. The B&O reached the Ohio River in 1852 and finished its branch from Cumberland, Md. to Pittsburgh by 1871.

The Western Maryland Railway (WM) started 30 years later as a small passenger railroad, heading northwest out of Baltimore. Its network grew and also started handling produce, freight, and mail. It reached Williamsport, Md. in 1873 to haul canal freight over the mountains.

The Western Maryland was purchased in 1902 by George Gould, son of the notorious financier Jay Gould, who envisioned a transcontinental railroad network from Baltimore to San

Trains still pass underneath the Western Maryland's Keystone Viaduct, near GAP Mile 30.

Photo: Matt Kerr

Francisco. While this vision was never fully achieved, Gould and his successors did extend the WM to Cumberland in 1906 and then to Connellsville, Pa. in 1912.

At Connellsville the Western Maryland connected to the Pittsburgh and Lake Erie Railroad (P&LE), which had built its Youghiogheny Branch from Pittsburgh in 1883 to tap the enormous coal and coke resources along the west bank of the Youghiogheny River.

The Western Maryland and P&LE paralleled the B&O all the way from Cumberland to Pittsburgh; at times the two railroads were little more than a stone's throw apart. The B&O's successor is CSX, the busy railroad whose tracks carry freight trains and Amtrak between Cumberland and Pittsburgh today.

After World War I, the B&O gained control of the Western Maryland, but due to federal regulations, still had to operate it as a separate – and competitive – line. This duplication of service was the good fortune that allowed for the creation of the Great Allegheny Passage.

The Western Maryland was one of the most efficient, best-run railroads in the country, but by the late 1960's, costs were rising and income was declining. Merger proceedings with the B&O were begun. In 1975, the Western Maryland was formally abandoned as a through-route, although short sections were retained to serve local coal mines well into the 1980's.

After the P&LE lost its connection with the Western Maryland at Connellsville, and the last big coal mine on the line closed in 1982, there was little traffic left. In 1991 the P&LE, too, was abandoned.

TRANSFORMATION TO TRAIL

The story of the Great Allegheny Passage begins June 1973. In that year George Leilich, vice president of the Western Maryland, testified before the Interstate Commerce Commission during the railway's abandonment hearing, and stated that the corridor could become a "nature and bicycle pathway." The abandonment request was granted in early 1975, with the Western Pennsylvania Conservancy (WPC) poised to acquire some of the corridor on behalf of the state.

Just as the Justice Douglas Hike had been used to draw attention to the canal and its recreational potential, Western Maryland officials and WPC organized a "last train ride" media event on May 21, 1975 to accomplish the same for this corridor.

Spectators watch the train cross bridge at Ohiopyle for the last time.

Photo: Paul g Wiegman

John Rex, Bureau of State Parks, receives the deed for the Western Maryland Railways corridor near Ohiopyle from John Oliver of the Western PA Conservancy, November 1978.

Photo: Paul g Wiegman

Dignitaries boarded a B&O train in Pittsburgh, and then switched to the Western Maryland near Dunbar. They saw first-hand what only railroaders had experienced – stunning landscapes from atop bold structures that crossed the Allegheny Mountains. The idea of converting the line to a recreational corridor was now an exciting possibility.

The official birth of the Great Allegheny Passage was on June 9, 1978, when, after years of imagining and planning, the WPC purchased 27 miles of the Western Maryland right-of-way. In November of that same year, the WPC sold it to the Pennsylvania's Bureau of State Parks. Soon after, Ohiopyle State Park superintendent Larry Adams quietly began converting the abandoned line to trail. Cobbling together resources, labor, and equipment, he constructed trail through the park, including the decking and railing on the Ohiopyle High Bridge. The first nine miles of trail from Ohiopyle to near Confluence were officially opened in 1986. Trail use grew steadily and so did the enthusiasm to build more miles.

In the 1980's and 90's, local residents formed trail groups, bounded by county or city lines, between Cumberland and Pittsburgh. With help from local governments and private foundations, they bought the abandoned rail lines and other properties needed to build additional segments of trail.

The groups formed the Allegheny Trail Alliance in 1995 to establish working relationships, develop system-wide guidelines, raise funds for construction, and market the world-class trail they were building. At that time, there were nearly 70 miles of trail yet to build and several major viaducts and tunnels to reconstruct for trail use. Support came from government, local communities, private foundations, and, above all, the volunteer groups that kept pushing to make the near-impossible happen.

In 2001, the trail groups chose the name the Great Allegheny Passage for the entire trail system. That same year, 100 continuous miles were completed from Meyersdale, Pa. to McKeesport, Pa. In 2006, the GAP connected to the C&O Canal Towpath in Cumberland, which earned the GAP the national honor of being the first inductee into the Rails-to-Trails Conservancy's Hall of Fame.

Construction took place between 2007 and 2013 on the nine-mile gap from McKeesport to the Pittsburgh city limits. This remarkable section was pieced together with over 30 separate properties and includes three bridges.

Today, the GAP runs nearly 150 miles from Cumberland to Pittsburgh, terminating at Point State Park. It took 35 years and over $80 million to build, thanks to the work of visionary leaders and thousands of volunteers along the way.

Cyclists, hikers, runners, trainspotters, birdwatchers, and history buffs now travel the C&O Canal Towpath and Great Allegheny Passage between Washington, D.C. and Pittsburgh, some for day trips and others for eight-day journeys. The next chapters will help you plan an amazing adventure.

Two new trail bridges were simultaneously set in place over Norfolk Southern's active rail lines in Whitaker and Duquesne, July 2010.

Photo: Linda Boxx

Aerial view of
Salisbury Viaduct
on the GAP.
Photo: US Aerial Video

PLAN YOUR JOURNEY

Traveling the C&O Canal Towpath and Great Allegheny Passage is a delight. Full of history, spectacular scenery, lovely trail towns, and expansive views, you can arrange all kinds of day trips, out-and-back overnights, or long-distance trips between Pittsburgh and Washington, D.C. You can ride one way for lunch and back for ice cream. You can carry your own gear or hire a shuttle service. You can camp under the stars in a hiker-biker Adirondack-style shelter, or you can treat yourself to plush surroundings and a fancy breakfast among the many guesthouses and B&B's along the trails. You can prep your own meals or take advantage of cafes, sandwich shops, inns, restaurants, and breweries for your sustenance.

Members of Black Girls Do Bike, Cleveland, Ohio Chapter, in Cumberland.

Photo: Doug Riegner

Hundreds of thousands of outdoor enthusiasts travel these trails each year, most by bike. How might you plan your next adventure? A variety of outfitters, tour companies, or trip-planning services (see page 231) can arrange it all for you. Or, review the FAQ's, lists, and itineraries that follow. Either way, gather some friends, and explore these beloved trails and the towns they connect.

Be safe, take photos, and enjoy your adventure!

FREQUENTLY ASKED QUESTIONS

ARE THE TRAILS ONLY FOR BIKING?

This section of *TrailGuide* is geared toward bicyclists, with an eye toward those planning overnight or thru-trips. But runners, walkers and hikers also enjoy both trails (they can connect to the Appalachian Trail and Laurel Highlands Hiking Trail, for example). Horseback riders can pick from selected sections of the GAP and C&O Canal Towpath, rollerbladers excel on paved sections near Pittsburgh and Washington, D.C., and cross-country skiers often take advantage of winter snow at higher elevations.

WHAT'S A GOOD PLACE TO START?

With scores of trailheads and places to park (see pages 40 and 41), you can start in any trail town for day trips or overnights. For those considering a multiday ride, pick few trail towns you'd like to visit and center your travels among those destinations. If you're considering a thru-trip, take a look at some itineraries we've laid out on pages 102-105.

IS IT BUMPY OR SMOOTH? IS IT HILLY OR FLAT?

The Great Allegheny Passage is largely rail-trail, evenly-topped with crushed limestone with a paved section in Connellsville and a 16.3-mile stretch between McKeesport and Downtown Pittsburgh. It's relatively smooth and easy to pedal, run, or hike. Over the 23.7 miles from Cumberland to the Eastern Continental Divide, it rises 1,767 feet steadily (less than two percent on average), enough to notice, but not so much to ruin the winding mountain views. From the Eastern Continental

Riders near
Confluence
on the GAP.

Photo:
Doug Riegner

Divide, 125.1 miles to Pittsburgh, it drops 1,680 feet imperceptibly (about 0.25 percent on average), making it feel like a light tailwind at times.

In contrast, the C&O Canal Towpath is nearly level, gaining only 605 feet from Washington, D.C. to Cumberland. However, since it was built for mules and foot traffic, cyclists, hikers, and runners find it slower going, with a mix of trail surfaces (a bit of hard-packed stone, some sections of freshly-laid limestone between miles 22 and 85, but largely two-track packed dirt, roots, and rocks) making for a bumpier journey.

WHAT ABOUT TRAFFIC?

The C&O Canal Towpath and GAP are non-motorized trails, and the only vehicles you should see are occasional authorized maintenance vehicles. Please note that there are some exceptions on the GAP where you will travel on a separated bike lane in both Connellsville and Munhall, via lightly traveled roads for a few blocks near and in McKeesport, and on a stretch of sidewalk in West Homestead. In Downtown Pittsburgh, the GAP runs on a dedicated bike/ped path along the Monongahela River, although an alternative route uses city streets for 0.75 miles (see page 222 for a map).

Thru-rider near Dam 5 on the C&O Canal Towpath.
Photo: Great Allegheny Passage Conservancy

HOW FAR IS IT BETWEEN TOWNS?

On the C&O Canal Towpath, you're in the woods for stretches of nearly 30 miles at a time, with abundant opportunities for camping. Trail towns are spaced apart, so planning your stops takes some advance planning. Conversely, you're never more than nine miles from a trail town on the GAP, giving you more options. See page six for a mileage chart. To set up overnights and meals, see pages 228-232.

WHAT KIND OF BIKE DO I NEED?

There are all kinds of bicycles that work well on the GAP, including touring bikes, hybrids, mountain bikes, cyclocross bikes, urban commuters, and department store specials. Even a road bike might work during dry weather. Tandems, trikes, and recumbents are quite popular. Fat bikes are unnecessary unless there's deep snow. A 28 mm tire or larger is your best bet.

On the C&O Canal Towpath, you'll want tires with some width (at least 32 mm) and grip. Many riders are glad to have a front suspension to ease the bumps. Road bikes are inadequate and trikes are cumbersome; neither are recommended. Know how to change a tire (bring a hand-pump and some spare tubes even on a day ride). Make sure your bike fits you properly by having a bike shop adjust your seat, handlebars, and brakes. For a list of bike shops and bike rentals along the way, see page 232.

WHAT ABOUT E-BIKES?

Only certain types of e-bikes are allowed, namely, two- or three-wheeled cycles with fully operating pedals, an electric motor of 750 watts or less, weighing less than 100 pounds and less than 36" wide. Throttle-assist e-bikes are not allowed on either trail, and neither are vehicles with combustion engines (except authorized maintenance vehicles). The speed limit for e-bikes is 15 miles per hour, the same as standard bicycles.

WHAT ABOUT ANIMALS?

Both the GAP and C&O Canal Towpath are dog-friendly. Please leash and control your pet, and remove pet waste. Pay special attention to other travelers, especially those approaching on bikes, to avoid injury. Horseback riding is permitted on certain sections of the C&O Canal Towpath, and adjacent to certain sections of the GAP. See www.gaptrail.org or www.nps.gov/choh for details. As for wildlife, look for groundhogs, rabbits, snakes, deer, and wild turkeys, all commonly seen.

IS THERE CELL COVERAGE?

While cell coverage is improving, you'll find some "dead zones" and you can't always count on getting good service. Take advantage of trail town stops to recharge your phone. Don't rely on USB-only cords, either; bring a cord with a complete wall plug. Hiker-biker campgrounds typically do not have electrical hookups, although some private campgrounds do.

WHERE CAN I FILL MY WATER BOTTLES?

Most trail town businesses will allow customers to fill their water bottles, and most (but not all) hiker-biker campgrounds have potable water available seasonally. Still, it's best to carry two bottles and to top them off whenever possible to stay hydrated and prepared. Thru-travelers may wish to carry a water filter or pump, especially on the C&O Canal Towpath.

HOW ABOUT BATHROOMS?

Aside from trail town businesses and visitor centers in towns, you may be limited to chemical toilets at hiker-biker campgrounds. You may wish to carry hand sanitizer in case options are limited.

AM I GOING TO GET WET OR MUDDY?

If you're out for a weekend or week-long adventure, you might find yourself traveling in a rain shower. A rain jacket will help keep you dry, but puddles or standing water (primarily on the C&O Canal Towpath) will splash your legs and "stripe" your back. Fenders can prevent this, of course, but they can also fill with caked-on mud after heavier rains.

Dodging the raindrops in Ohiopyle State Park.

Photo: Great Allegheny Passage Conservancy

HOW DO I TRANSPORT MY GEAR?

For day-trippers, you likely don't need more than a trunk bag for a hand pump, spare tube, bike tools, snacks, perhaps a jacket, and your phone and keys. For overnight and thru-trippers, it all depends on how much gear you have, and whether you're camping or staying in overnight lodging.

The Whitaker Flyover between Homestead and Duquesne.

Photo: Paul g Wiegman

If you're carrying baggage on your bike, you may consider a trunk bag and a handlebar bag, and/or saddlebags on your rear or front racks. Some cyclists use trailers, although the bumpier and narrower C&O Canal Towpath can be a challenge for trailers with two wheels. Hikers will want a backpack that can carry between 30 and 65 liters of gear, and you'll want boots or trail shoes that fit well.

If you would like to travel light, you can hire a shuttle service, tour operator, or outfitter to haul your bags from town to town. (If you're camping, keep in mind that most hiker-biker campgrounds are not accessible by shuttle service or car.) See page 231 for a listing of bicycle tour operators and transportation services.

HOW FAR CAN I TRAVEL EACH DAY?

Most cyclists can average eight to ten miles an hour, but it depends on how many stops you'd like to make for snacks, photo ops, and exploring. Day-trippers with lighter loads can often move more quickly. Most overnight and thru-riders tackle between 35 and 60 miles a day, half before lunch and half after lunch, depending on their destination. On the GAP, towns are between 10 and 20 miles apart, so there are places to stop and refuel. On the C&O Canal Towpath, you'll need to be able to ride 30 miles between some towns.

WHERE CAN I STAY?

There are all kinds of options along both trails for overnight lodging. The GAP is known for its B&B's, guesthouses, hostels, inns, and hotels, from fancy to modest. Much of the GAP is along private land, so you cannot camp "just anywhere." However, there are both hiker-biker and private campgrounds along the way to make camping easy for bicyclists. Hikers will need to blend indoor and outdoor lodging to avoid long days.

The C&O Canal Towpath is known for hiker-biker (and some nearby private) campgrounds every few miles, making it easy to start and end your day at your convenience. While there are fewer trail towns, each of them have B&B's, inns, and guesthouses that cater to trail travelers. Note that some trail towns are a few miles off the trail via some on-road travel.

If you're planning to stay at hotels, inns, B&B's, or hostels, you'll want to make reservations in advance. Hiker-biker campsites are officially first-come, first-served, and seldom full, but be prepared to travel further in case all sites are taken. Hiker-biker campgrounds often limit group sizes to six per campsite. For a list of campgrounds, see pages 38-39. For lodging options, see page 230.

Heading out from a plush bed-and-breakfast.

Photo: Pam Lantz

WHAT ABOUT MEALS?

Trail towns feature a mix of restaurants, cafes, diners, and speciality shops like distilleries and breweries. Some will have one or two options; most will have several to choose from. You can often pick up snacks and groceries in towns, as well. Please note that some restaurants have limited hours on Sundays and Mondays, so it's best to call ahead for hours. If you're camping and handling your own meals, packing a small cooking set and propane stove is a foolproof way to make sure you have a hot meal. For a list of restaurants on both trails, see page 231.

WHAT ELSE IS THERE TO DO IN TOWNS?

All kinds of things! Music festivals, art crawls, bike loops, neighborhood walks, farmers' markets, parades, historical tours, cemetery walks, Friday night football, or just a quiet evening on the porch of your B&B. Chat up a local at a restaurant. Pick up a piece of gear at a bike shop. Stroll by the river.

WHAT ABOUT GROUPS?

Groups are welcome on both trails. For groups over 25 on the GAP, please contact the Great Allegheny Passage Conservancy at admin@gaptrail.org for permits. Additionally, keep in mind that most trail town lodging and restaurants aren't accustomed to large groups without reservations. You may need to split up among several lodging partners or restaurants. We do encourage you to spend your money at local businesses rather than bringing in mobile food trailers from outside the region.

Traveling group at a B&B.

Photo: Teresa Danley

WHAT ABOUT FOOTWEAR?

For cyclists, you'll be fine with a pair of sneakers, or whatever shoes you normally ride in. Bring an extra pair of "town shoes" or "camp shoes" for once you're off your bike. For hikers or runners, a trail shoe is perfect for both trails, provided you have sandals for knocking around your campsite or hotel.

WHAT IF MY BIKE BREAKS?

It's best if you (or someone in your group) knows how – and has the tools – to fix a flat tire, a broken chain link, or a loose seatpost. A roll of duct tape and some zip ties can provide a temporary fix to other issues. Some trail towns have full-service bike shops (see the list on page 232) and along the GAP, there are fix-it stations with pumps and tools, placed strategically.

HOW DO I SET UP RETURN TRANSPORTATION?

Consider renting a minivan or SUV for a one-way return trip at the end of your trip. Your best options are the major car rental companies in Pittsburgh, Cumberland, and Washington, D.C.

You can also use Amtrak's Capitol Limited (see page 36), which provides one-way service among several trail towns along both the GAP and C&O Canal Towpath, as well as Pittsburgh and Washington, D.C. For an extra $20, you can reserve a place to transport your bike in a dedicated slot. Bicycle slots are limited, so make your reservation well in advance of your trip.

Your best bet might be to hire a shuttle service, tour operator, or outfitter to take you from your endpoint back to your car. Of course, you can hire a service to provide just the shuttle or to take care of planning the entire trip. There are several outfitters and tour operators who offer a variety of packaged or flexible trips on both trails. See page 231 for a listing of bicycle tour operators and transportation services.

Crossing the Dunbar Creek Viaduct on the GAP.

Photo: Great Allegheny Passage Conservancy

ANY TIPS FOR FLYING IN TO THE REGION?
Commercial airlines serve Pittsburgh and Washington, D.C., and both have trail connections to their respective airports.

From the Pittsburgh International Airport there is a marked 6.3 mile bicycle route on low-usage airport and public roads, ending at the Montour Trail. From there, you can take an 18.0 mile (primarily road) ride to the GAP in Downtown Pittsburgh, or a 43.5 mile (primarily trail) ride to the GAP at McKeesport. For more information, visit www.montourtrail.org. Alternatively, take the 28X Airport Flyer, which runs directly to Downtown Pittsburgh every half hour, and stops near the western terminus of the GAP. Each bus has a rack for two standard bikes. For details, visit www.portauthority.org.

Landing at Washington D.C.'s Reagan National Airport allows you to ride the adjacent Mount Vernon Trail about five miles north to the Francis Scott Key Bridge, where you'll cross the Potomac River. At the end of the bridge, bear immediately right onto the asphalt path that passes around the small Francis Scott Key Memorial and take the mule crossover bridge down to the C&O Canal Towpath, in the city's Georgetown neighborhood. For details, visit www.wmata.com. Alternatively, take the D.C. Metrorail's Blue Line from the airport to Rosslyn, which is a short distance from the Francis Scott Key Bridge. Two bicycles are permitted per car except during weekday rush hours.

Just a note that other than in Pittsburgh or Washington, D.C., it's unlikely you'll find a ride-sharing service anywhere.

Pausing along the C&O Canal Towpath for lunch.
Photo: Great Allegheny Passage Conservancy

GO WITH THE PROS

Every year, thousands of travelers opt for hiring an outfitter, tour operator, or shuttle service to make a trip on the Great Allegheny Passage or C&O Canal Towpath a perfect biking or hiking vacation. Most are based in Pittsburgh, Washington, D.C., or in trail towns in between. All offer expert, personalized attention. Commonly-offered services include the following:

TRIP PACKAGES:
Some tour companies offer a variety of pre-planned, self-guided trip packages with daily mileage and overnight lodging booked ahead of time. Most trips are in the three- to eight-day range.

CUSTOM ITINERARIES:
Others will design your crew's custom day-by-day itinerary, making it possible to add a whitewater outing, day hike, museum stop, or architecture tour if you like.

GUIDED ADVENTURES:
Some outfitters will run scheduled guided trips with seasoned experts pedaling alongside you and other guests, and a van carrying your gear to the next stop.

RELIABLE GEAR:
Most will equip you and your traveling companions with trail-ready bicycles sized to fit, usually with racks, saddlebags, and a helmet. Of course, you can always use your own bike if you wish.

SHUTTLES AND TRANSPORTATION:
There are several vendors that provide luggage shuttling and/or return transportation as their primary service, and others that incorporate these services into their trip packages and custom itineraries.

Services vary by business, so we recommend that you contact them in advance to better understand the options each offers. Start with the list on page 231.

TRAVEL SAFELY

HOURS:
The Great Allegheny Passage and C&O Canal Towpath are open from dawn to dusk. You may want a headlamp for tunnels, but plan on daylight travel only. While both trails are open year-round, the Big Savage Tunnel on the GAP is closed from late November to early April. There is no detour.

SPEED LIMIT AND COMMON COURTESY:
The speed limit on both trails is 15 miles per hour. Please travel single file and stay to the right. Give a friendly audible signal in advance of passing, pass slowly and courteously on the left, and only when it is safe to do so.

Bicyclists must yield the right of way to hikers, walkers, and equestrians. Walk bikes over aqueducts and unlit tunnels. Take extra caution and slow down when the trail surface is slippery or crowded. Give extra space to younger, older, or less-experienced travelers.

Stop at all railroad and street crossings, and watch for bollards, vehicles and uneven trail surfaces. Take extra care along short sections of trail that follow shared roadways. On the GAP, stay on the trail surface and please respect adjacent property, most of which is privately-owned.

HELMETS, E-BIKES, AND WHEELCHAIRS:
By Pennsylvania state law, bicyclists under the age of 12 must wear helmets. In Maryland, everyone under 16 (and in Montgomery County, under 18) must wear a helmet. We recommend them for everyone.

Wheelchairs and similar devices built specifically for mobility disabilities are allowed on the GAP and C&O Canal Towpath.

Only certain types of e-bikes are allowed, namely, two- or three- wheeled cycles with fully operating pedals, an electric motor of 750 watts or less, weighing less than 100 pounds and less than 36" wide. Throttle-assist e-bikes are not allowed on either trail, and neither are vehicles with combustion engines (except authorized maintenance vehicles).

CAMPING, FIRES, ALCOHOL, AND LEAVE NO TRACE:
No fires or camping are allowed, except in designated hiker-biker campgrounds. No alcohol is permitted on either trail. Dispose of your waste properly, leave what you find, and be considerate of other visitors.

EMERGENCIES:
Carry a first aid kit. Call 911 in case of an emergency. Always alert a friend to your intended plans.

ALL ABOARD
AMTRAK

Amtrak offers bicycle service on the Capitol Limited, which runs between Chicago and Washington, D.C., through Toledo, Ohio, and Cleveland, with trailside stops in Pittsburgh, Connellsville, Pa., Cumberland, Md., Martinsburg, W.Va., Harpers Ferry, W.Va., and Rockville, Md. For an extra $20 on top of the regular fare, you can secure your bicycle in a retrofitted baggage car and get on or off at any station. Each train has room for eight bikes.

Great for making an end-to-end tour possible, this service can also facilitate fun weekend trips. For example, you can leave from Union Station in Washington D.C. around 4:00 pm on a Friday, get off at Harpers Ferry, and ride back over the weekend. Alternatively, the 88.8 miles between Cumberland and Connellsville make a very enjoyable two or three day journey, with a train ride back to your car.

Visit www.gaptrail.org to see a video on how to use the racks. Amtrak staff members cannot help you load your bicycle, but are helpful and friendly. It's a good idea to take heavy bags off your bicycle since your front wheel will be carrying all the weight. There are shelves in the baggage car where you can leave your bags. If you wish to pack your partially disassembled bicycle as checked luggage – allowed in Chicago, Toledo, Cleveland, Pittsburgh and Washington D.C. – boxes are usually available for purchase at the station.

**AMTRAK STATIONS
CLOSE TO THE TRAILS**

Pittsburgh (PGH)
1100 Liberty Ave

Connellsville (COV)
400 Water St

Cumberland (CUM)
201 E Harrison St

Harpers Ferry (HFY)
112 Potomac St

Washington, DC (WAS)
50 Massachusetts Ave, NE.

AMTRAK SCHEDULE

29 departure	◀ Train Number ▶	30 departure
4:05 PM	Washington, DC	------------
4:29 PM	Rockville, MD	12:16 PM
5:16 PM	Harpers Ferry, WV	11:31 AM
5:45 PM	Martinsburg, WV	11:01 AM
7:24 PM	Cumberland, MD	9:32 AM
9:47 PM	Connellsville, PA	6:59 AM
11:59 PM	Pittsburgh, PA	5:20 AM

Amtrak may reduce service on the Capitol Limited from daily service to three days weekly during the winter months.

Check www.amtrak.com for current schedules, delays or service disruption.

PACKING LIST

OUTERWEAR
- Padded cycling shorts
- Cycling gloves and helmet
- Warm shirt or windbreaker
- Rain jacket, fleece hat
- Synthetic or wool socks (2-3 pairs)
- Wicking-fabric t-shirts or jerseys with pockets
- Clothes for lodging or camping
- Long-sleeved shirt and pants

Plan for the weather and season. If you're camping, be sure to bring clothes for layering during chilly nights.

CAMPING GEAR
- Tent or bivy with tarp/rainfly
- Sleeping bag *(down is best)*
- Backpacking stove with fuel
- Cooking kit, utensils
- Water filter or iodine
- Food *(carry an extra meal)*
- Sleeping pad *(closed cell are lighter)*
- Ground cover
- Matches or lighter
- Sheet or sleeping bag liner
- Extra Ziploc bags
- Clothesline or nylon rope

Pack as light as you can, and split gear among those with whom you're traveling.

TOOLS AND BIKE PARTS
- Mini-pump
- Tire levers and patch kit
- Headlight or flashlight*
- Small set of Allen wrenches
- Bungee cords
- Bike lock
- Spare tube and spokes for your wheel
- Screwdriver
- Leatherman or pocket knife
- Chain tool
- Duct tape, zip ties, and rubber bands

*For finding your guesthouse after dinner, at your campsite, or for traveling through unlit tunnels.

DON'T FORGET!
- Identification
- Cell phone and charger
- Water bottles/hydration pack
- Snacks or trail mix
- Sunblock and lip balm
- Bug spray
- First aid kit
- Toilet paper
- Keys
- Hand sanitizer
- Cash and credit cards
- Plastic bags
- Sunglasses
- Toiletries, Chamois cream
- *TrailGuide*

CAMPING OPTIONS

⇥ Hiker-Biker Overnight Campgrounds (No Fee) ⇤

There are 31 hiker-biker campgrounds located along the C&O Canal Towpath and four along the GAP. There is no fee to use them and they are available on a first-come, first-served basis. None are accessible by car.

Stays are limited to one night per site, per trip. All sites have nearby pit toilets, picnic tables, and grills. Potable water is often available from April 15 to November 15, but is not guaranteed at each location.

For more information on hiker-biker, drive-in, or group camping along the C&O CanalTowpath: www.nps.gov/choh/planyourvisit/camping.htm.

C&O MILE 16.6 – **Swains Lock**
C&O MILE 26.1 – **Horsepen Branch**
C&O MILE 30.5 – **Chisel Branch**
C&O MILE 34.4 – **Turtle Run**
C&O MILE 38.2 – **Marble Quarry**
C&O MILE 42.5 – **Indian Flats**
C&O MILE 47.6 – **Calico Rocks**
C&O MILE 50.3 – **Bald Eagle Island**
C&O MILE 62.9 – **Huckleberry Hill**
C&O MILE 75.2 – **Killiansburg Cave**
C&O MILE 79.2 – **Horseshoe Bend**
C&O MILE 82.7 – **Big Woods**
C&O MILE 90.9 – **Opequon Junction**
C&O MILE 95.2 – **Cumberland Valley**
C&O MILE 101.2 – **Jordan Junction**
C&O MILE 110 – **North Mountain**
C&O MILE 116 – **Licking Creek**
C&O MILE 120.6 – **Little Pool**

C&O MILE 126 – **White Rock**
C&O MILE 129.9 – **Leopards Mill**
C&O MILE 133.6 – **Cacapon Junction**
C&O MILE 139.2 – **Indigo Neck**
C&O MILE 144.5 – **Devil's Alley**
C&O MILE 149.4 – **Stickpile Hill**
C&O MILE 154.1 – **Sorrel Ridge**
C&O MILE 157.4 – **Purslane Run**
C&O MILE 162.1 – **Town Creek**
C&O MILE 164.8 – **Potomac Forks**
C&O MILE 169.1 – **Pigmans Ferry**
C&O MILE 175.3 – **Iron's Mountain**
C&O MILE 180.1 – **Evitts Creek**
GAP MILE 89.4 – **Connellsville***
GAP MILE 99.6 – **Roundbottom***
GAP MILE 110.2 – **Cedar Creek Park***
GAP MILE 122.6 – **Dravo's Landing**

* with Adirondack shelters

⇢ Commercial Campgrounds (Fee) ⇠

C&O MILE 11.5 – NPS Marsden Tract (Civic and Scout Groups Only) Six walk-in group sites (30 people each) with picnic tables and fire pits. Pit toilets. Potable water available April 15 - November 15. No parking on site. Must make reservations at www.recreation.gov; $40/night.

C&O MILE 54 – Brunswick Family Campground 65 RV and 300 tent sites, pavilions and picnic tables, electric service and water hookups, bath house with hot showers, boat ramp. 301-834-9950.

C&O MILE 69.4 – NPS Antietam Creek Campground Twenty walk-in sites with picnic table, grill, and fire pit; each site can accommodate eight people. Pit toilets. Potable water available April 15-November 15. Must make reservations at www.recreation.gov; $10/night.

C&O MILE 110.4 – NPS McCoys Ferry Campground Twelve drive-in sites with picnic table, grill, and fire pit; each site can accommodate eight people. Pit toilets. Potable water available April 15-October 31. One group site (30 people max) is available. Must make reservations at www. recreation.gov; $20/night.

C&O MILE 140.9 – NPS Fifteen Mile Creek Campground Nine drive-in sites with picnic table, grill, and fire pit; each site can accommodate eight people. Pit toilets. Potable water available April 15-November 15. One group site (30 people max) is available. Must make reservations at www. recreation.gov; $20/night.

C&O MILE 141 – Little Orleans Campground 0.25 mile from the towpath. 301-478-2325

C&O MILE 156 – NPS Paw Paw Tunnel Campground Ten walk-in sites with picnic table, grill, and fire pit; each site can accommodate eight people. Pit toilets. Potable water available April 15-November 15. Must make reservations at www.recreation.gov; $20/night.

C&O MILE 173.3 – NPS Spring Gap Campground Twelve drive-in sites with picnic table, grill, and fire pit; each site can accommodate eight people. Pit toilets. Potable water available April 15-November 15. Two group sites (30 people each) are available. Must make reservations at www. recreation.gov; $20/night.

GAP MILE 0.0 – Cumberland YMCA Camping 1.1 miles from GAP mile 0 in Cumberland; access to indoor showers and potable water during business hours. 301-777-9622.

GAP MILE 15.5 - Trail Inn Campground Frostburg. Showers, towels provided, picnic tables, grills, bike wash, potable water, coin-operated laundry. May 1 to October 31. 301-689-6466.

GAP MILE 31.9 – Maple Festival Park Primitive Camping Meyersdale. Restrooms with showers. Approximately May 1 to October 31. 814-634-0213

GAP MILE 43.7 – Husky Haven Campground Rockwood. Picnic tables, firewood, chemical toilets, Open approximately April 15 to October 31. Bath houses, bike wash. 814-926-2024.

GAP MILE 61.4 – Youghiogheny River Dam Outflow Campground Confluence. 200 feet from the trail. Tent sites with fire rings. Restroom facilities, hot showers, potable water. Mid-May to early October. 814-395-3242.

GAP MILE 61 – Paddler's Lane Campground Two flat miles from Confluence. 30 sites, picnic tables, fire rings, firewood, chemical toilets, bath houses, potable water. 814-964-0410

GAP MILE 72.6 – Ohiopyle State Park Take the marked side trail just north of Ohiopyle High Bridge near mile 73 up a steep hill to Kentuck Knob Campground. A new hiker-biker campground right on the GAP will open sometime in 2022. April to December. Call 888-PA-PARKS for reservations.

GAP MILE 92.0 – KOA at River's Edge Adelaide. Tent sites with picnic tables and fire rings; restroom facilities, hot showers. Laundry, convenience store, swimming pool. Full-service cabins-reservations required. 724-628-4880

GAP MILE 110.3 – Cedar Creek Park Campground Two campgrounds - One for groups (fee), and the other for trail and river users (free). Restroom facilities, potable water. Reservations required for groups. 724-830-3950, ext. 0.

GAP MILE 114.1 – GAP Trail Campground, LLC West Newton. Free Wifi, hot showers. 724-244-5859 or www.gaptrailcampground.com

WHERE TO PARK

Washington, D.C. (fee)
(C&O Mile 1.0)
Weekend street parking on K
Street, or in one of Georgetown's
parking garages

Great Falls Tavern (fee)
(C&O Mile 14.4)
11710 MacArthur Boulevard
Potomac, MD 20854

Seneca Creek Aqueduct
(C&O Mile 22.7)
11001 Rileys Lock Road
Darnstown, MD 20874

White's Ferry
(C&O Mile 35.5)
24801 Whites Ferry Road
Dickerson, MD 20842

Brunswick, MD 21716
(C&O Mile 55.0)
MARC train station parking lot
100 South Maple Avenue

Harpers Ferry, WV 25425 (fee)
(C&O Mile 60.7)
Harpers Ferry Visitors Center
171 Shoreline Drive

Shepherdstown, WV 25443
(C&O Mile 72.8)
NPS parking lot
16389 Canal Road
Sharpsburg, MD 21782

Williamsport, MD 21795
(C&O Mile 99.4)
NPS Visitors Center parking lot
205 West Potomac Street

Fort Frederick State Park
(C&O Mile 114.5)
11100 Fort Frederick Road
Big Pool, MD 21711

Hancock, MD 21750
(C&O Mile 124.1)
Western Md. Rail Trail parking lot
256 East Main Street

Little Orleans, MD 21766
(C&O Mile 140.9)
11001 High Germany Road

Paw Paw Tunnel Campground
(C&O Mile 156.1)
MD-51 near Malcolm Road SE,
Oldtown, MD 21555

Oldtown, MD 21555
(C&O Mile 166.7)
Green Spring Road SE

Spring Gap Campground
(C&O Mile 173.3)
MD-51 near Kirk Hollow Road
Oldtown, MD 21555

Cumberland, MD 21502
(C&O 184.5/GAP 0.0)
13 Canal Street (fee, short term)
or 16 Howard Street (free, long
term)

Cash Valley Road
(GAP Mile 5.2)
11250 Cash Valley Road NW
La Vale, MD 21502

Frostburg, MD 21532
(GAP Mile 15.5)
20 Depot Street or
10200 New Hope Road NW

Eastern Continental Divide
(GAP Mile 24.6)
1765 Deal Road
Meyersdale, PA 15552

Meyersdale, PA 15552
(GAP Mile 31.9)
527 Main Street

Garrett, PA 15542
(GAP Mile 36.5)
1787 Berlin Street

Rockwood, PA 15557
(GAP Mile 43.8)
131 Rockdale Road

Confluence, PA 15424
(GAP Mile 61.3)
855 River Road
or 479 Ram Cat Road

Ohiopyle, PA 15470
(GAP Mile 71.9)
7 Sheridan Street or
Ferncliff Parking area

Connellsville, PA 15425
(GAP Mile 89.0)
Front Street (Yough River Park) or
794 Vanderbilt Road

Whitsett, PA 15473
(GAP Mile 104.1)
First Street/Weiss Memorial Park

Smithton Beach Road
(GAP Mile 108.1)
Smithton Beach Road
Belle Vernon, PA 15012

Cedar Creek Park
(GAP Mile 110.3)
453 Evergreen Drive
Belle Vernon, PA 15012

West Newton, PA 15089
(GAP Mile 114.1)
111 Collinsburg Road

Boston, PA 15135
(GAP Mile 128.2)
1906 Donner Street
McKeesport, PA 15135

McKeesport, PA 15132
(GAP Mile 132.5)
501 Water Street

Homestead, PA 15120
(GAP Mile 140.5)
192 East Waterfront Drive

Pittsburgh's South Side (fee)
(GAP Mile 145.2)
Ladle Parking Garage
2640 Sidney Street
Pittsburgh, PA 15203

Downtown Pittsburgh (fee)
(GAP mile 147.8)
First Avenue Garage and T Station
600 First Avenue
Pittsburgh, PA 15222
or
Grant Street Transportation Center
55 11th Street
Pittsburgh, PA 15219

*Visit www.gaptrail.org for
additional locations and up-to-date
overnight availability.*

Overnight Parking: *Overnight parking is limited to certain locations, and
you'll likely pay for it in Downtown Pittsburgh, on Pittsburgh's South Side,
and in Georgetown (or anywhere around Washington, D.C.), whether you're
parking for the day or overnight. If you plan to park overnight, we suggest
notifying local police or a nearby visitor center to alert them. This may prevent
them from starting a search-and-rescue operation or towing your car. For
fee-based parking garages, you may need to complete a form showing your
intended return date. If using an NPS parking lot for extended use, please
check NPS.gov and complete the C&O Parking Permit Request form.*

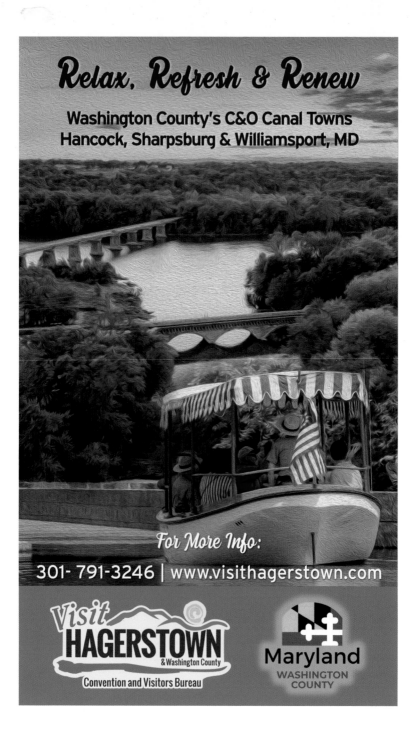

Relax, Refresh & Renew

Washington County's C&O Canal Towns
Hancock, Sharpsburg & Williamsport, MD

For More Info:
301- 791-3246 | www.visithagerstown.com

Visit
HAGERSTOWN
& Washington County
Convention and Visitors Bureau

Maryland
WASHINGTON COUNTY

MILE BY MILE
C&O CANAL TOWPATH

POINTS OF INTEREST

MILE 0.0 - Tidelock: The Canal starts at the mouth of Rock Creek behind the Thompson Boat Center; a granite marker designates the first lock of the canal system. See page 109 for details on finding Mile Zero.

MILE 0.4 - Georgetown Visitor Center: The site of a bust commemorating Supreme Court Justice William Douglas. His 1954 hike was a major event in the saving of the canal from being paved as a parkway. For a description of Georgetown, see pages 106-107. The visitor center is closed for the 2022 season.

MILE 0.9 - Towpath cross-over bridge at 34th Street carries the Towpath to the river side of the canal where it remains as it makes its way to Cumberland.

MILE 1.1 - The remains of the **Alexandria Canal's Potomac Aqueduct** that once connected the C&O Canal to a canal in Virginia, leading to the port of Alexandria.

Bicyclists riding in Great Falls Park.

Photo: Doug Riegner

GREAT FALLS TAVERN

The **Great Falls Tavern** was built first in 1828 as a simple stone locktender's house. The design for all early lockhouses included a kitchen and parlor downstairs and two bedrooms upstairs.

Great Falls became a popular destination. A decade of prosperity for both the C&O Canal and the Tavern followed the Civil War. Over 500 boats a year carrying coal, lumber, grains, and other raw materials passed the Tavern on their way to the ports of Georgetown and Alexandria.

This era of success and affluence for the C&O Canal ceased in the 1880's and disaster arrived in 1889. A wall of water from heavy rains, part of the same storm that caused the Johnstown Flood, came crashing down the Potomac River and submerged much of the canal. Flood waters lapped at the second floor of the Great Falls Tavern.

When the waters receded, the 60 year old building stood witness to the devastation. Whole sections of the canal and its towpath were damaged by the river. Canal boats, lockhouses, and many masonry structures were smashed or washed away. The Chesapeake and Ohio Canal lay in ruin and the company faced possible bankruptcy.

On the eve of foreclosure the canal was protected by trustees for the owners of canal repair bonds issued in 1844 and in 1878 – the majority of the latter owned by its former great rival, the Baltimore and Ohio Railroad. The trustees agreed to repair the canal and continue to operate it, reopening the canal in September 1891. Although the C&O Canal and the Great Falls Tavern persevered to conduct business for the next three decades, the prosperous days of the 1870's were history.

Great Falls Tavern. Photo: Great Allegheny Passage Conservancy

MILE 1.5 - Access to the **Capital Crescent Trail:** Built on the former Georgetown Branch of the B&O Railroad, this trail closely parallels the canal for 1.7 miles before it heads up the paved trail to Bethesda, Md.

MILE 2.3 - **Inclined Plane:** Built to raise and lower boats between the canal and the Potomac River to bypass the four locks leading to the Rock Creek basin.

MILE 3.2 - **Fletchers Boat House** and the **Abner Cloud House:** Rent canoes, kayaks, and bikes at the boat house at Fletchers Cove. The Abner Cloud House, built in 1801, is the oldest house along the canal. Just west is the cross-over bridge of the Capital Crescent Trail which heads to Bethesda.

MILE 5.6 - Visit the site, near Lock 6, where **President John Quincy Adams** broke ground for the C&O Canal on July 4, 1828.

MILE 7.6 - **Clara Barton House** and **Glen Echo Park:** These two National Park Service sites are about a half-mile from the Towpath.

MILE 8.3 - 9.5 - **Seven Locks:** Starting with Lock 8, this series of locks is located in close succession over 1¼ mile to raise the canal 56 feet.

MILE 12.3 - **Widewater:** Canal builders utilized part of the old river channel, here nearly 500 feet wide. They built a guard wall to dam up water for navigation and carry the towpath. The Potomac River in flood remembers its ancient course and has many times breached the wall, requiring towpath travelers to use the "Berma" Road detour.

MILE 13.6 - 14.4 - **Six Locks:** Starting with Lock 15, in less than a mile these six locks were built to create an elevation change of 49 feet around the Great Falls. Lock 15 features a picturesque log wall built to simulate the historic appearance of the stone-filled log cribbing walls originally used here.

Trail Conditions and Alerts for the C&O Canal Towpath:
Visit www.nps.gov/choh/planyourvisit/conditions.htm

Visitors admire the falls from the overlook. Take the short trail just past Mile 14.

Photo: John Urman

MILE 14.1 - Great Falls Tavern and Overlook: Great Falls, the most spectacular natural landmark in the Washington, D.C. metropolitan area, consists of cascading rapids and several 20-foot waterfalls over a series of jagged rocks, with a total 76-foot drop in elevation over a distance of less than a mile. The Potomac River narrows from nearly 1,000 feet, just above the falls, to between 60 and 100 feet wide as it rushes through Mather Gorge. The Great Falls of the Potomac displays the steepest and most spectacular fall line rapids of any eastern river. This dramatic scene is a popular site with local residents and tourists from around the world.

MILE 14.4 - Great Falls Tavern Visitor Center: Normally open Wednesday through Sunday, 9:00 am to 4:30 pm, with nearby bathrooms and picnic tables. Trails in the area lead to the remains of the Maryland Gold Mine which operated in the area during the late 19th and early 20th centuries.

MILE 16.6 - Swains Lock: Alternate free parking area for accessing Great Falls by bicycle. Horseback riding is permitted from here west to Cumberland.

MILE 22.8 - Seneca Creek Aqueduct: Built with three 33-foot span arches, this aqueduct carries the canal over the Seneca River. Constructed from stone from the nearby quarry, the same red sandstone was used to build the Smithsonian Castle on the National Mall. Its upstream arch collapsed in a localized flood in 1971 and a bridge spans the gap. The bracing stabilizes the remaining part of the aqueduct.

This aqueduct is unique in that it and Lock 24 are designed as one continuous structure. A boat headed upstream would enter directly into the aqueduct as it exited the lock, passing through its upstream gate. A boat headed downstream would have to wait above the aqueduct if the lock was not ready for it, entering the aqueduct only when it could pass directly into the lock at the other end.

Note the lower towpath wing fence and post with a line carved into it and the date 1889, indicating the high water mark of the great flood that put the canal company into bankruptcy.

MILE 22.8 - Riley's Lockhouse: Open most weekends in the spring and fall. Volunteers dressed in period clothing lead tours of the lockhouse. For information, call 301-384-8584.

Lockhouse at Seneca Creek.

Photo: Great Allegheny Passage Conservancy

MILE 31.9 - Broad Run Trunk: First constructed as a double culvert for Broad Run, this was later converted into the canal's only wooden aqueduct.

MILE 35.5 - White's Ferry: For over a century, this was the last operating cable ferry on the Potomac River, once used by farmers to get their crops to market. A legal dispute shuttered ferry service in 2021 and it remains up to local landowners, proprietors, and government officials to determine if it will reopen, making a unique way to cross the Potomac for the short road ride to Leesburg, Va.

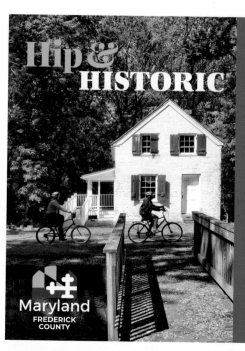
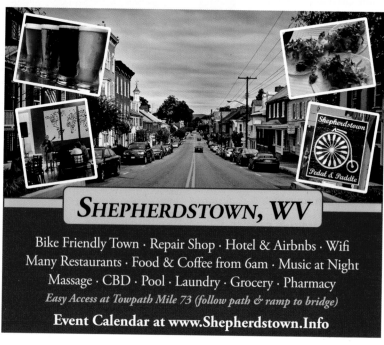

MILE 35.5 - Leesburg: Located just across the Potomac River in Virginia's horse country, the picturesque town of Leesburg is rich in history and culture and has many fine restaurants and bike-friendly places to stay.

Once in Leesburg, you can explore the county by bicycle. Check out Ball's Bluff Battlefield Regional Park, which preserves the site of the Battle of Ball's Bluff, the largest Civil War engagement to take place in Loudoun County.

Ball's Bluff Battlefield Park, Leesburg.

Photo: Julie McCool, FuninFairfaxVA.com

The popular Washington & Old Dominion rail trail runs through Leesburg, and the entire 45-mile trail is paved. It ends in Alexandria, Va. and, combined with the towpath, makes a nice loop ride between Washington, D.C. and Leesburg. For a map, see: www.bikewashington.org.

MILE 42.2 - Monocacy Aqueduct: With its seven support arches, it is the longest of the 11 stone aqueducts and a very dramatic structure. The aqueduct is 516 foot long and has seven 54-foot span arches.

The Aqueduct was stabilized in 2005. A number of components were left as they were for interpretive reasons. The iron railing on the east end shows the marks of the tow ropes, pulling their heavy loads, rubbing against it. Note the twisted bit of railing beside the Towpath at mid-aqueduct. It bears witness to the force of flood waters and the debris they carry when the floods are high enough to overtop the aqueduct and batter railings. The contemporary railings are designed to be readily removed when a flood is coming so they will not catch and hold debris, becoming damaged and contributing to the stress placed on the aqueduct.

No longer "swayback" since the reconstruction of the aqueduct.

Photo: Steve Dean

MILE 48.4 - Point of Rocks Tunnel: Canal construction above here was prohibited until the spring of 1832 due to a right-of-way dispute with the B&O Railroad. In May 1833 a compromise between the two companies resulted in both systems passing through four narrow areas with the use of tunnels and the building up of land beside the river using stone blasted from the hillsides to create space for the canal. After canal operations ceased, the railroad laid track over part of the canal bed in some of these narrow areas.

MILE 50.9 - Lander Lockhouse: Open for touring during weekends in the summer, this lockhouse is positioned at Lock 29, and is near a boat ramp for access to the Potomac River.

MILE 51.5 - Catoctin Creek Aqueduct: Called the "Crooked Aqueduct" because of the bend at the upstream end, it was also considered by canallers as the most beautiful of all the aqueducts because of the scenic approaches that the curves helped to create. The elliptical center arch was not as structurally strong as the flanking semicircle arches and began sagging in the early 1900's. Two of the aqueduct's three arches collapsed during a fall flood in 1973. Major reconstruction of this aqueduct was completed by the National Park Service in 2011 at a cost of $3.9 million.

MILE 55.0 - Brunswick: Cross the tracks and head for the friendly town of Brunswick (see pages 110-113 for a profile and town map) for an appealing mix of old fashioned ambiance and sophisticated retail. The restored Queen Anne-style train station greets you as you head into town.

MILE 60.7 - Harpers Ferry/Bolivar: These towns and the Harpers Ferry National Historical Park that envelop them are rich in Civil War history and feature museums, restaurants, walking tours, and beautiful vistas. See pages 118-121 for a profile and town map. The Appalachian Trail winds through Harpers Ferry, past John Brown's Fort, Jefferson Rock, and the grounds of Storer College.

MILE 69.4 - Antietam Creek Aqueduct: This aqueduct is unique for its three elliptical arches, designed with two smaller 28-foot side arches flanking the center 40-foot arch.

MILE 72.8 - Shepherdstown: Follow a footpath to the switchback ramp that leads you up and over the bridge into Shepherdstown, West Virginia, chartered as Mecklenburg, Virginia, in 1762. A college town with a delightful business district filled with coffee shops, restaurants, and lodging options, Shepherdstown is a perfect overnight stop. See pages 124-127 for a profile and town map.

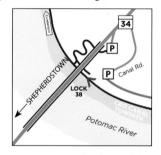

St Peter's Catholic Church in historic Harpers Ferry.

MILE 76.8 - Sharpsburg: At Snyders Landing, you can leave the towpath and make a short on-road climb to the town of Sharpsburg, Md., where 23,000 Union and Confederate troops were killed, wounded, or unaccounted for on September 17, 1862, the bloodiest single-day battle in American history.

On September 22, confident following the Union victory at the Battle of Antietam, President Abraham Lincoln issued a preliminary Emancipation Proclamation, declaring that as of January 1, 1863, all slaves in the rebellious states "shall be then, thenceforward, and forever free." While the Emancipation Proclamation did not free a single slave, it was an important turning point in the war, transforming the fight to preserve the nation into a battle for human freedom. (History.com)

From *Harper's Weekly*, 1862: Burnside Bridge in Sharpsburg.

To tour Antietam National Battlefield, the town of Sharpsburg, and the Burnside Bridge, please see the map on page 96 for a slightly hilly, on-road loop.

MILE 84.4 - Guard Gate: The winch house was used to raise and lower beams to close the opening in the guard wall that allows the canal to pass through it. The guard wall extended from the land side of the canal to the dam abutment and another guard wall ran from the dam abutment up to Inlet Lock 4. Today the trail is on the guard wall along the river, and the historic towpath beside the canal is not maintained for most of that distance.

McMahon's Mill.

Photo: Bonnachoven/ Wikimedia Commons

MILE 85.6 - Big Slackwater: Here, 2.7 miles of the towpath were renovated in 2012 and eliminated the need for the long-standing road detour. The $19 million restoration project included drilling into bedrock and erecting a series of concrete bridges along the river, alternating with sections of historically-accurate towpath. Dam No. 4 created a pool in the river which allowed the canal builders to use the river channel.

MILE 88.1 - McMahon's Mill: Originally constructed as a grist mill and later used to generate electricity.

MILE 99.4 - Railroad Lift Bridge: Built in 1923 by the Western Maryland Railway, this distinctive railroad lift bridge was designed to operate like an elevator, lowering the railroad tracks vertically across the canal to allow trains to deliver coal to a nearby power plant. It was only used from June of 1923 until the canal was closed to navigation in May of 1924 after the floods in the spring of that year. Trains supplying coal to the Potomac Edison Power plant used this bridge until the line was abandoned in the 1980's. Although short, at just 40 feet long, and designed with a simple Warren truss overhead structure, it has a certain engineering elegance. Raised to a fixed position, it now carries bicyclists and pedestrians across the watered canal into Williamsport.

Railroad Lift Bridge carries bicyclists and pedestrians into Williamsport.

Photo: Great Allegheny Passage Conservancy

Floating on the newly-reconstructed Conococheague Aqueduct.

Photo: Maggie Clingan

MILE 99.4 - Williamsport: This canal town features a beautiful historic district with a bed-and-breakfast, taverns, shopping, and eateries. See pages 130-133 for a profile and town map. Inside the historic Cushwa Warehouse is the Williamsport Visitor Center, open March to November, Wednesday through Sunday, 9:00 am to 4:30 pm. Nearby is the new headquarters for the C&O Canal National Historic Park, which opened in 2021.

MILE 99.8 - Conococheague Aqueduct: Just beyond the Cushwa Basin is the Conococheague Aqueduct. This long aqueduct has three 60-foot arches and is best known for the story of its lost upstream wall. Early in the morning of April 29, 1920, the wall collapsed as a boat was entering the aqueduct, sending it into the river below with water flowing out from the canal. The mules were saved by the captain's quick-thinking son when he released them from the towline in response to his father's call to do so. Captain Frank Myers, who had been at the tiller, was able to jump to the aqueduct's intact abutment wall.

The aqueduct was the target of Confederate efforts to disrupt canal operations. On August 4, 1863, their army tore down part of its wall and ripped out a large hole in one of the arches. Again on July 18, 1864, large parapet stones were torn out. These areas are identifiable today by their smaller stones at the west end on the towpath side.

MILE 106.6 - Dam 5: Dam 5 provided the water for 18 miles of the canal. It is a stone masonry dam with an early-20th century hydro-electric plant on the West Virginia side. The half-mile slackwater navigation section behind Dam 5 is known as **Little Slackwater**. At one time a mule bridge spanned the canal to continue the towpath along the river bank above the inlet lock. A part of the path is located on a wide ledge carved into the cliff that even major floods have not been able to damage.

The spillway is a popular place to fish.

Photo: John Urman

MILE 108.8 through **109** - **Four Locks:** This series of locks allowed boats to take a shortcut across Prather's Neck, rather than follow a four-mile bend in the river. Several historic buildings still remain. Lockhouse 49 is available for overnight lodging through the C&O Canal Trust's Canal Quarters program.

Photo: Joe Nichols

MILE 112.1 - Fort Frederick State Park: This French and Indian War fort is about 0.3 miles from the towpath. Built in 1756 for Maryland's frontier defense during the French and Indian War (1754-1763), the fort's stone wall and two barracks have been restored to their 1758 appearance. Historic displays are in the fort, barracks and visitor center. Fort Frederick was unique because of its large size and strong stone wall. During the Civil War, Union troops were often stationed around the fort to guard the C&O Canal.

MILE 113 - The **Western Maryland Rail Trail:** Begins one mile west of Fort Frederick and parallels the C&O Canal Towpath for 26 miles to Little Orleans, Md. See map on page 98.

MILE 116.1 - Licking Creek Aqueduct: The largest of the six single-arch aqueducts between here and Cumberland, the Licking Creek Aqueduct has a 90-foot span.

Tolonoway Creek Aqueduct.

Photo: Keld Wichmann Moeller

MILE 123 - Tonoloway Creek Aqueduct: This aqueduct was constructed in a manner that used the natural rock formation on the west bank of the Great Tonoloway Creek as the abutment. The result is a semicircular, irregular arch with a span of 53 feet that would have been 80 feet if fully developed. The poor quality stone used in this aqueduct created problems and necessitated substantial repairs until the 1880's when most of the top of the aqueduct was removed and replaced with a concrete and wooden flume, and a wooden towpath bridge.

MILE 124.1 - Hancock: With ample lodging, an outfitter and bike shop, and restaurants known for locally-baked pies, Hancock hugs the Potomac River and serves as a great hub for overnight and out-and-back cycling adventures on the C&O Canal Towpath and the Western Maryland Rail-Trail. See pages 136-139 for a profile and town map, and page 99 for a suggested day ride itinerary.

Early snow near Hancock.

Photo: Steve Dean

Remnants of Round Top Cement Mill.

Photo: Sam Urman

MILE 127.4 - Round Top Cement Mill: The arches along the rock face were limestone kilns used to produce cement.

MILE 136.6 - Sideling Hill Creek Aqueduct: : This aqueduct has a single, elliptical 60-foot span. The pool behind Dam 6 once extended the 2.5 miles up the river to Sideling Hill Creek, raising the water levels some 13 feet above where they are now. A waste weir is on the berm at the east end of the aqueduct. Due to the berm wall collapse, the aqueduct was given a timber trunk in 1874.

Sideling Hill Creek's torturous route is the boundary between Maryland's Washington and Allegany Counties. Its 104-square-mile watershed is of exceptional value, rich in biological diversity.

MILE 140.9 - Fifteenmile Creek Aqueduct: This aqueduct has a single, semicircular arch with a 50-foot span and is missing its berm parapet. This aqueduct is flanked by campgrounds and is exceptionally scenic at any time of the year. Fifteenmile Creek was named because it is about 15 miles up the Potomac from Hancock and about 15 miles down the Potomac from Oldtown for riders on the rugged trail that

The single-arched Fifteenmile Creek Aqueduct near Little Orleans.

Photo: Jeffrey Muller

was developed in the 1750's to connect Fort Frederick (below Hancock) and Fort Cumberland (at Wills Creek). Today the Oldtown Road that crosses the creek about 1/3rd of a mile upstream from the aqueduct preserves much of that route.

MILE 154.5 - **Lock 63 1/3** and **Lock 64 2/3**: When building the canal, the company decided that they could leave out one lock by building locks 62 through 66 with a 10-foot lift rather than an eight-foot lift. Instead of renumbering locks upstream, they numbered these two locks with fractions and skipped Lock 65.

Lock 64 2/3 along the C&O Canal Towpath.

Photo: Steve Dean

Two Great Locations Off the C&O Canal

WE LOVE CYCLISTS

Paw Paw, West Virginia – Mile 156.2
Oldtown, Maryland – Mile 166.7

Canal Cabins, Paw Paw, WV
143 Louie's Lane, Paw Paw, WV

- Closest to Canal
- Self check-in at your pace
- Free laundry
- Bike wash
- Hot showers
- Free firewood
- French press
- Free Internet

Lock 70 Schoolhouse Inn, Oldtown, Maryland
19210 Opessa St, Oldtown, MD

- Sleeps group of six
- Self check-in at your pace
- Hot shower
- Coffee
- Bike wash
- Inside bike parking
- Free Internet
- Restaurant on site (School House Kitchen) owned separately

More info and both locations can be reserved at
www.canalcabins.com

MILE 155.2 to 155.8 - Paw Paw Tunnel: This engineering wonder was lined with nearly six million bricks, all hand-laid. Enjoy cooler temperatures as you pass through. If the tunnel is closed for repairs, which may be scheduled for 2022, you can walk your bike over the top using the two-mile Tunnel Hill Trail, which goes from portal to portal, with multiple switchbacks on the western side. Parking is available at the Paw Paw Tunnel access area off Maryland Route 51.

Photo: Great Allegheny Passage Conservancy

MILE 162.4 - Town Creek Aqueduct: This aqueduct crosses a waterway once called Old Town Creek. In 1838, the original contractor for the aqueduct, Willis Hatch, absconded when he received a scheduled partial payment from the canal company. He not only left the work incomplete, but also left his laborers and suppliers unpaid. Such events were not uncommon in the 19th century, and represent one of the major reasons for the labor unrest and violence that was such a significant part of the canal's construction history.

MILE 166.7 - Oldtown: Oldtown was built on the site of an abandoned Shawnee village at an important river crossing used by Native Americans and early frontiersmen. Its most famous son was English-born Thomas Cresap, who settled in Oldtown in 1741. Cresap gained a fearsome reputation as colonial border ruffian when he unsuccessfully tried to settle German immigrants on lands disputed by Pennsylvania and Maryland. Known as the "Maryland Monster," Cresap was tried in Philadelphia for his actions and paraded on the streets unrepentant, proclaiming, "This is one of prettiest towns in Maryland!" Mason and Dixon would finally resolve this dispute in 1767 with their famous survey.

Cresap's outpost became an important stop-over, for natives and colonists, including George Washington whose Ohio Company needed trade routes over the mountains. His son Michael's house remains today, operated as a private museum. It is open by appointment May through October.

MILE 175.7 - Lockhouse 75: This two-story lockhouse was reconstructed in 1978 and features interesting interpretive displays. It is open to the public and staffed by C&O Canal Association volunteers weekends from Memorial Day to Labor Day. Check with the Cumberland Visitor Center for current schedule.

Lockhouse 75.

Photo: Steve Dean

MILE 180.7 - Evitts Creek Aqueduct: At 70 feet, this is the shortest of the six single-arch aqueducts. The aqueduct is in poor condition despite stabilization efforts by the Park Service in 1979 and 1983.

Evitts Creek Aqueduct.

Photo: Paul Graunke

Pausing inside
Knobley Tunnel,
near Cumberland,
Md.

Photo: Doug Riegner

MILE 183 - Knobley Tunnel Trail: Five timber-lined tunnels were built by the Western Maryland Railroad during the Cumberland extension as it headed west from Hagerstown, Md. The first and longest is Indigo Tunnel, located near C&O 138, about a mile east of Little Orleans, and measures 4,350 feet. It is now closed to the public to protect endangered bat colonies in the tunnel. The Knobley Tunnel is 1,448 feet long and is the only one of these five open. It is part of an 0.8 mile rail-trail that crosses the Potomac River and then passes through Knobley Mountain into Carpendale, W.Va.

MILE 184.5 - Cumberland: This hub city was a busy inland port during the canal era, with two basins, wharves and facilities to load cargo onto waiting railcars and canal boats, and boatyards for boat-building. Much of this area is now occupied by the Canal Place development, with many shops, restaurants, and historical memorabilia. See pages 142-145 for a profile and town map,

The short trestle walk trail, built on part of an abandoned spur line that served the canal, leads from the towpath, across an elevated walkway that sweeps down into the heart of Canal Place and Mile Zero of the Great Allegheny Passage.

The 1924 flood that closed the canal to navigation and the devastating 1936 flood each caused significant damage to Cumberland. Flood control improvements were completed in 1959 by the U.S. Army Corps of Engineers. Dam 8 was removed and levees replaced the final mile of the canal and towpath. The towpath was rebuilt on the levee and sits about 30 feet higher than it had originally.

The Little Basin (closer to Will's Creek) had been acquired by the Western Maryland Railway in 1912 and filled to build their railroad and the beautiful station that today serves as the NPS visitor center and the station for the Western Maryland Scenic Railroad.

MILE 184.5 - **Canal Terminus:** The western end of the C&O Canal is marked by a granite post and is a popular spot for a picture to commemorate the towpath journey.

It can be accessed by a short switchback that begins about 100 yards before the trestle walk trail to Canal Place. After crossing railroad tracks, you can follow this pathway which passes under the trestle walk bridge and then follows the short reconstructed section of canal to the final mile marker.

Mile marker 184.5 with Canal Place in background, Cumberland.

Photo: Linda Boxx

GET BACK TO YOUR OWN PATH

60,000 acres of majestic nature, internationally recognized bike trails, three centuries of American history, a diverse food, brewery, and winery scene, and an endless amount of outdoor adventure. Get back to Mountain Maryland.

MARYLAND HERITAGE AREA
Maryland Heritage Areas Authority

ALLEGANY COUNTY
MOUNTAIN SIDE OF MARYLAND

MDMOUNTAIN**SIDE**.COM

MILE BY MILE
GREAT ALLEGHENY PASSAGE

The Youghiogheny River in Ohiopyle State Park.

Photo: Great Allegheny Passage Conservancy

POINTS OF INTEREST

MILE 0.0 – Cumberland: The quintessential canal and trail town, Cumberland is a commercial and cultural hub that caters to long-distance travelers. See pages 142-145 for a profile and town map. The Cumberland Visitor Center is located in the historic 1913 Western Maryland Railway Station at 13 Canal Street, in Canal Place. Normally, it is open seven days a week from 9:00 am to 5:00 pm. Mile Zero of the Great Allegheny Passage is marked by a medallion out front. After crossing Baltimore Street, heading up the GAP, you'll travel through the Cumberland Narrows, cut over the millennia by Wills Creek. At the top of Wills Mountain is a prominent outcropping known as Lover's Leap.

MILE 1.5 – Route 40 Bridge: This is the first of several through truss bridges built for the Western Maryland Railway Company. It consists of two 150-foot spans and was built to cross Braddock Run and the National Road, now Route 40.

Trail Conditions and Alerts for the Great Allegheny Passage:
Visit www.gaptrail.org/updates

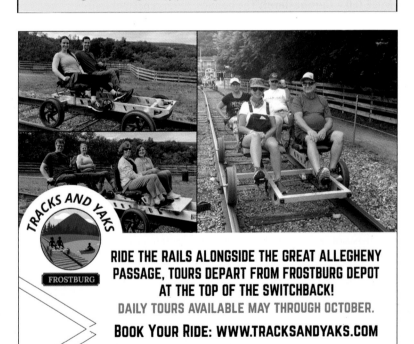

MILE 4.0 - **Bone Cave:** In 1912 workers excavating a cut for the Western Maryland Railway broke into a partly filled cave along the western slope of Wills Mountain on the outskirts of Cumberland. The Smithsonian Institution conducted an excavation between 1912 and 1916. Of the 41 genera of mammals found, approximately 16 percent are extinct today.

Enough bones were found to reconstruct skeletons for the Pleistocene cave bear and a saber-toothed cat, which are on permanent exhibit in the Ice Age Mammal exhibit at the National Museum of Natural History in Washington, D.C. Many of the fossilized bones date from 200,000 years ago. Bone Cave represents one of the finest Pleistocene-era faunas known from eastern North America. The remains of the cave can be seen on the walls and top of the cut.

MILE 5.3 - **Helmstetter's Curve:** This famous railroad landmark is a sweeping 180-degree horseshoe curve. It is named for the family whose farm it bisects and is a favorite spot for photographers and rail enthusiasts alike.

Western Maryland Railroad powers through Helmstetter's Curve.

Photo courtesy of the William P. Price Collection at the Lewis J. Ort Library, Frostburg State University. Frostburg , MD.

BIG SAVAGE TUNNEL

The promise of coal traffic sparked the Western Maryland Railway's ambitious westward extension of track in from Cumberland to Connellsville, 88 miles away, across the mountains. In that stretch, engineers designed four tunnels (and more than 20 bridges) to shorten the route and lessen the grade.

Constructing a 3,294-foot tunnel through Big Savage Mountain proved very difficult, as workers encountered a river of soft, wet mud and sand 600 feet from the western portal. Conventional airlock methods used to build subways in New York City helped stem the flow, as did "sand hogs," trained laborers who specialized in working in pressurized situations. Engineers selected state-of-the-art construction methods to complete **Big Savage Tunnel** in 1912, lining it with concrete to protect against rock falls.

Still, soft material continued to plague the railway, requiring continual repairs to the tunnel for decades. The Western Maryland finally abandoned the line in 1975, and the tunnel was closed and deteriorated.

In the late 1990's, the Allegheny Trail Alliance garnered support to restore and reopen the Big Savage Tunnel to complete the GAP. Work included extensive rock-bolting of the existing liner and installation of a new liner with an aggressive drainage system to minimize the freeze/thaw conditions that damaged the tunnel in the past.

The renovated tunnel is now the longest former railroad structure on the GAP. Work was completed in late 2003 at a cost of nearly $12 million. Donors are recognized on a monument at the Deal, Pa. access area, a few miles away.

Please note that **Big Savage Tunnel** is closed during the winter months to protect the tunnel lining from freezing temperatures, from late November to early April. Please see www.gaptrail.org for current information.

MILE 6.5 - Brush Tunnel: Shortest of the two concrete-lined tunnels in Maryland, this lighted tunnel was opened for use in 2006. Trail users share it with the Western Maryland Scenic Railroad train.

MILE 15.5 - Frostburg: The switchback uphill from the Frostburg trailhead takes you easily to the renovated Frostburg Depot Station. The scenic railroad from Cumberland runs from May to December, and a highlight of the trip is watching the turntable in action. Take the steps from the depot up into town; it's worth the climb. See pages 150-153 for a profile and town map.

MILE 17.9 - Borden Tunnel: Climbing up toward the state line on the trail, you'll encounter the 957-foot Borden Tunnel, along one of the quietest sections of the GAP. New motion-control lights installed in 2021 will guide your way through the tunnel, but slow down and use caution all the same.

Scott Cawood's bike themed sculpture welcomes travelers to Frostburg.

Photo: Great Allegheny Passage Conservancy

MILE 20.5 - Mason & Dixon Line: Colonial Maryland and Pennsylvania both claimed lands south of the 40th parallel. In the mid-1730's, the border conflicts erupted into violence between settlers claiming various loyalties to Maryland and Pennsylvania. An English team of Charles Mason and Jeremiah Dixon was commissioned to survey the boundaries between the colonies as part of the resolution of the dispute. The line was surveyed between 1763 and 1767 and proved to be a feat of remarkable accuracy. This famous line bears their names.

MILE 22.0 - Big Savage Tunnel: Less than two miles north of the state line is Big Savage Tunnel, the longest tunnel on this trip. The tunnel is closed during the winter months, from late November to early April. Please see www.gaptrail.org for current status.

Murals enhances the high point of the trail.

Photo: Larry Brock

MILE 23.7 - Eastern Continental Divide: Beyond the tunnel, a short climb brings you to an elevation of 2,392 feet above sea level and the Eastern Continental Divide, the boundary between the watersheds of the Atlantic Ocean and the Gulf of Mexico. You are at the highest point of the Pittsburgh-to-Washington D.C. journey. With murals depicting the history of the region and its railroads – and a short underpass in case you're caught in the rain! – this is a popular spot for photos.

MILE 29.8 - Keystone Viaduct: This 910-foot long, elegantly curved, combination truss bridge/deck plate girder viaduct was completed in 2003. A unique feature of its conversion was the use of iron oxide pigment from a nearby mine drainage treatment facility to tint the concrete. Understanding that the iron in the truss structure would stain the concrete decking, the trail builders decided to give the inevitable coloring process a head start.

Bollman Bridge, an ornately-engineered bridge repurposed for the GAP..

Photo: Great Allegheny Passage Conservancy

MILE 30.3 - Bollman Bridge: This iron bridge was originally built by the B&O Railroad to cross Gladdens Run in Bedford County. It was moved to Somerset County over 100 years ago to serve as a farm road crossing over the railroad. In 2007 it was again relocated to have a new life on the trail. This early example of a cast and wrought iron bridge was developed by master bridge engineer Wendell Bollman.

MILE 31.9- Meyersdale: This charming town, known for its Maple Festival, offers B&B's, guesthouses, an inn, restaurants, a library, and convenience and drugstores. See pages 160-163 for a profile and town map. The Meyersdale Area Historical Society has renovated the Western Maryland Station, providing a welcome center for trail users, with displays on local history as well as a retail store that benefits the local historical society.

Meyersdale Area Historical Society museum and visitor center.

Photo: Great Allegheny Passage Conservancy

MILE 33.7 - Salisbury Viaduct: One of the most distinctive structures on the Great Allegheny Passage, the Salisbury Viaduct, at 1,908 feet long, dominates the valley. The 101-foot-high steel trestle was a key engineering achievement for the Western Maryland Railway Company's Connellsville Extension.

Disaster struck during the building of viaduct on July 10, 1911 when an electric traveling crane crashed to the ground while lifting a 14.5 ton girder. Six men were killed and one seriously injured. A month later, another worker died when he fell off the deck.

Abandoned for railroad use in the early 1980's, it was decked for trail use in the spring of 1999. Sweeping views of the former B&O Railroad (now CSX) can be enjoyed from the viaduct.

Farmhouse in Garrett along the Casselman River.

Photo: Great Allegheny Passage Conservancy

MILE 36.5 - Garrett: From Meyersdale to Garrett, you're out of the woods and into farmlands, including wind farms, Somerset County's newest energy industry. About five miles north of Garrett is the Wymp's Gap Fossil Quarry. You'll see a marker labeled GR-5. School classes come here to dig fossils and learn about local geology. In Garrett, the September 11th National Memorial Trail heads north to the Flight 93 National Memorial. For details, visit www.911trail.org.

MILE 43.8 - Rockwood: A visitors center offers information, water, and the only cell signal amplifier on the trail. The town of Rockwood is across the river from the trail. See page 168-171 for a profile and town map. Bed-and-breakfasts, a guesthouse, and hostel are available for overnighters.

MILE 50.0 - Markleton: Across the bridge and downstream from the local post office was the site of the Markleton Sanitarium, built first as a mountain resort reachable by rail and later used as a restorative clinic for tuberculosis patients. For a short time it housed German prisoners of war. It was destroyed by fire in 1903 and its foundation is still noticeable at ground level. Markleton was once the site of the world's largest wood pulp mill which closed in 1893. Much of the pulp was shipped to a paper mill in West Newton, Pa.

Bicyclists on the Pinkerton Low Bridge.

Photo: Doug Riegner

MILE 51.9 - Pinkerton Bridges, Tunnel, and Horn: There were once two railroad tunnels built through the Pinkerton Horn, a narrow pinch of erosion-resistant land that created a peninsula in the Casselman River.

The first was the B&O tunnel, completed in 1871. Like many railroad tunnels of that era, it was lined with timber. When it was destroyed by fire in 1879, a bypass, or "shoofly," was built around the horn until the tunnel could be repaired.

CSX completed a construction project in 2014 to open-cut the B&O tunnel to accommodate double-stacked rail cars. The fill from this massive cut was placed on top of the Pinkerton horn and has drastically changed the way this area looks.

The Western Maryland built its tunnel in 1912, flanked by the Pinkerton Low and High Bridges over the Casselman River. It had not been open to trail use until 2015 due to its severely deteriorated condition. The GAP had used the B&O shoofly for a scenic 1.5 mile bypass around the Pinkerton horn.

Major work was undertaken in 2015 to reline the Western Maryland tunnel, making it safe for trail use. It is a spectacular feature, with the bridge-tunnel-bridge in quick succession. The Pinkerton Tunnel Bypass remains a scenic option.

SAVING FERNCLIFF

For decades, **Ferncliff Peninsula** provided respite for residents of Ohiopyle, Pa. and visitors who walked its woods and swam at its beaches. A place of natural beauty, it was also home to dozens of extremely rare plant species. When plans were unveiled in the late 1940's to timber the land and build an amusement park, one persistent woman took action.

Lillian McCahan, station agent for the Western Maryland Railway in Ohiopyle, wrote countless letters to public and private officials, including a Pittsburgh commission that was to become the Western Pennsylvania Conservancy (WPC), pleading for help to protect this special place. With donations from retail magnate Edgar J. Kaufmann (his country home Fallingwater was nearby) and the Andrew W. Mellon Foundation, the 100-acre peninsula was obtained by the WPC in 1951 to resell to the state.

Lillian McCahan worried that Ohiopyle had "fallen off the tourism map" and worked to reverse that trend.

Photo: courtesy of Marci McGuinness

To create a state park, though, much more land would be needed. Much to Ms. McCahan's dismay, the WPC began buying properties in Ohiopyle and large tracts in surrounding Stewart Township, making land unavailable for mining, farming and other activities vital to the local economy.

She wrote hundreds of pages of letters to try to stop what she was sure would be the death of Ohiopyle, then a town of about 400 residents. Many local people felt forced to sell their homes or farms, fearing that if they did not accept the WPC's offer, the state would condemn their property at a lesser value. As a result, Ms. McCahan became a bitter opponent to the creation of the state park, an ironic twist since she had worked so hard to call attention to the special treasure of Ferncliff.

In 1978 the WPC acquired part of the abandoned Western Maryland Railway to add to Ohiopyle State Park, which would become the first section of the Great Allegheny Passage.

MILE 61.6 - Confluence: Occupying the peninsulas among the Casselman and Youghiogheny Rivers and Laurel Hill Creek, Confluence boasts a collection of lovely B&B's, a bike shop, and several restaurants. See pages 174-177 for a profile and town map. From here to Whitsett, Pa., is one of Pennsylvania's Important Bird Areas, designated by the National Audubon Society.

As you leave Confluence, heading west, you will travel eleven miles to Ohiopyle, along the oldest and most popular section of trail.

MILE 63.3 - Ohiopyle State Park: Named among the top ten state parks in the country by *Camping Life* magazine, Ohiopyle is one of the most visited parks in Pennsylvania. Ohiopyle State Park, with its 20,633 acres, features whitewater rafting, many camping venues, an array of trails, mature forests, stunning waterfalls and breathtaking views of the Youghiogheny River gorge. As you meander through Ohiopyle State Park along the trail among the wildflowers and trees, you can enjoy watching fishermen, rafters, and kayakers. In several areas, you can easily access the river to picnic on the banks or on boulders in the river.

Riding through Pennsylvania's deepest gorge inside Ohiopyle State Park.

Photo: Great Allegheny Passage Conservancy

Ohiopyle Falls and Visitor Center.

Photo: US Aerial Video

MILE 71.9 - Ohiopyle: As you come into the village of Ohiopyle, a former train station serves as a trail visitor center, and the new education center overlooking the falls is certainly worth a visit. See pages 182-185 for a profile and town map. George Washington was forced to turn back here on his first visit in 1753, declaring the river unnavigable because of the waterfalls. The area above the falls is popular for wading and just cooling off on a hot day. The GAP continues across Ohiopyle Low Bridge to Ferncliff Peninsula, a National Natural Landmark with rare plant species able to survive because the falls and the rapids that encircle the peninsula moderate the temperature extremes. Ohiopyle High Bridge, at the other end of the peninsula, is a favorite spot for watching the rafters in the rapids far below.

MILE 79.3 - Yough River Gorge Overlook: The scenic vista and boulder seat make this spot a natural for a water break and photo. The view shows the western side of the Youghiogheny River Gorge, Pennsylvania's deepest gorge. The backdrop is made more scenic because of the meander in the river caused by the outwash from Johnson Run and Bruner Run. The large boulders in the river are almost all from the same sandstone that also forms the falls at Ohiopyle.

MILE 87.1 - Bowest Junction and the Sheepskin Trail:
Bowest is short for the B&O – Western Maryland Junction
where the Western Maryland spur served mines in West
Virginia. The first two miles have been converted into the
Sheepskin Trail and lead to the small town of Dunbar. In
the 1790's, iron furnace operations marked the beginning of
what would become Dunbar's lifeblood over the next century.
Connellsville Street is the main road through town and the
remaining buildings stand as a testament to a more prosperous
time.

MILE 88.8 - Connellsville: This trail town boasts amazing
architecture, historic churches, an array of restaurants and
lodging, and public art to enjoy on side trips. Amtrak serves
Connellsville, and trail access and parking are available at
Yough River Park. See pages 188-191 for a profile and town
map. Stop by the Connellsville Canteen for a detailed model
train exhibit.

Thru-riders at
Connellsville
Hiker-Biker
Campground.

Photo: Great Allegheny
Passage Conservancy

COAL, COKE & CALAMITY

The famed "Connellsville Coalfield" ran under what is now the GAP from Ohiopyle State Park to Adalaide, Pa., and for 45 miles north and south. The coal was soft, easily mined, in a pure seam 10 feet thick, and was regarded as some of the highest-quality metallurgical coal in the world. Coal mined from this region was baked in airless ovens into coke, which in turn fired the country's iron- and steel-producing industry centered in Pittsburgh. By the 1910's, at the height of the industrial revolution, one ninth of the country's coal mining took place within a few miles of Connellsville, and over 40,000 beehive and rectangular ovens lit up the night sky with an orange-red glow. Today, you can see several abandoned ovens along the GAP near Adalaide, Pa.

Coal mining was a dangerous activity, dark, crowded, and at risk of cave-ins and explosions. The worst mining disaster in Pennsylvania history occurred in 1907 near the village of Van Meter, Pa., when 239 coal miners were killed in a massive underground explosion at the Darr mine; only one man escaped. National attention was brought to the conditions in the mines after this disaster. As a result, the federal government initiated efforts to prevent mining accidents beginning in 1908 and established the U.S. Bureau of Mines in 1910. There is a memorial to the miners killed in the Darr mine near GAP mile marker 105.

Workers pose in front of coke ovens, c. 1890.

Photo Courtesy of Coal and Coke Heritage Center, Penn State Fayette.

MILE 92.0 - Adelaide: This coke-producing company town, named for industrialist Henry Clay Frick's wife, was developed during the heyday of Pennsylvania's coal and coke industry. Several batteries of coke ovens still stand near GAP mile 93.5. Look only; they are on private property.

The remains of Old Overholt Distillery are just across the river, near GAP mile 91. Whiskey-making was a thriving cottage industry well into the nineteenth century. Nearly every farm had a still. Monongahela Rye became an internationally recognized whiskey in the early 1800's.

MILE 94.6- **Dawson:** Cross the river to experience the Dawson National Historic District with the Victorian-style homes of the coal and coke baron Cochran family and the Philip G. Cochran Memorial United Methodist Church, resplendent with Tiffany windows, an amazing organ, and handsome woodwork.

MILE 102.9 - Layton and Perryopolis: George Washington was a principal landowner in the area and established an early mill complex at Perryopolis, across the river from Layton. His complex included a grist mill and a distillery. The grist mill has been restored. Local clay deposits were used to make bricks for the coke ovens.

MILE 104.1 - Whitsett:
This town achieved National Historic Register of Historic Places status in 1995 as it exemplified the typical coal patch company town. Going north, you'll pass the remains of the Pittsburgh Coal Company's Banning Number One Mine, and overhead you'll see the impressive Pittsburgh & West Virginia Banning trestle. Only concrete foundations and silos remain of the once-extensive mining complex that included a coal cleaning plant and rows of company houses.

The Ruins Project, Whitsett.

Photo: Bryan M. Perry

RAILROAD RELICS

The Great Allegheny Passage features a treasure trove of preserved railroad structures once built to support train travel along the Western Maryland Railway, Pittsburgh and Lake Erie Railroad, and Union Railroad.

► Between Connellsville and Boston, you'll see a handful of remaining whistle posts, placed a quarter-mile in advance of road crossings, prompting the locomotive engineer to sound a whistle alerting travelers to its presence.

◄ This concrete phone booth – built to withstand time and elements – was moved from a nearby spur to its present location in Meyersdale. Prior to radio communication, trains would stop at intervals awaiting orders to proceed, and the engineer would reach the dispatcher by manually connecting a phone to the overhead wires that ran parallel to the tracks.

► The last remaining 40-foot "shorty" boxcar in the P&LE's system now stands preserved in Boston. It was built in 1929 and restored in 2010.

MILE 108.1- Smithton:
With a wide "beach" along the Youghiogheny River, Smithton gives outdoor enthusiasts access to fishing and paddlesports. It was once a mill town supporting the region's coal mining, coke ovens, and transportation of goods produced along nearby Jacobs Creek – like Pennsylvania's famous rye whiskey. For nearly 100 years, Jones Brewing Company produced Stoney's Beer right in town. Today, an artwork-laden pollinator garden and a charming bed-and-breakfast entice trail travelers.

MILE 110.3 - Cedar Creek Park: The GAP passes through Westmoreland County's 479-acre park along the Youghiogheny River. The park provides river access, picnic pavilions, permanent restrooms, a primitive biker/hiker campground, and group camping sites. The Cedar Creek Gorge walking trail is home to rare wildflowers in the spring and makes an enjoyable nature walk year-round.

Reflective garden and rest stop in Smithton.
Photo: Great Allegheny Passage Conservancy

MILE 114.1 - West Newton: Astride the Youghiogheny River, West Newton boasts several B&B's, a bike shop, bakery, restaurants, and a new distillery. See pages 196-199 for a profile and town map. Stop in the West Newton Station for information from friendly volunteers, GAP merchandise, and a rest stop in the lovely replica of the 1910 P&LE train station that once stood there. Check out the walls of the meeting room, which house an eclectic collection of historic signs from hiking and biking trails from across the U.S.

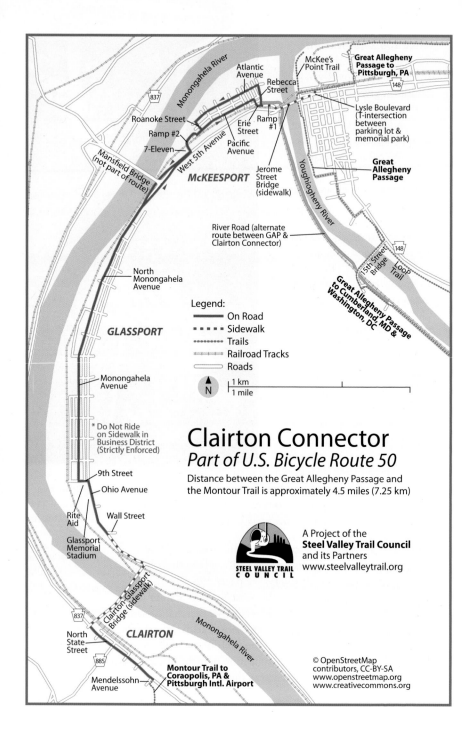

Monongahela River

837

McKee's Point Trail

Great Allegheny Passage to Pittsburgh, PA

148

Atlantic Avenue

Rebecca Street

Lysle Boulevard (T-intersection between parking lot & memorial park)

Roanoke Street

Erie Street

Ramp #1

Ramp #2

Pacific Avenue

7-Eleven

West 5th Avenue

Jerome Street Bridge (sidewalk)

Great Allegheny Passage

Mansfield Bridge (not part of route)

McKEESPORT

Youghiogheny River

River Road (alternate route between GAP & Clairton Connector)

North Monongahela Avenue

15th Street Bridge

148

Loop Trail

Great Allegheny Passage to Cumberland, MD & Washington, DC

GLASSPORT

Monongahela Avenue

Legend:

━━━ On Road
▪ ▪ ▪ ▪ Sidewalk
•••••••• Trails
╫╫╫╫╫ Railroad Tracks
⬭ Roads

▲ N

1 km
1 mile

* Do Not Ride on Sidewalk in Business District (Strictly Enforced)

9th Street

Ohio Avenue

Rite Aid

Wall Street

Glassport Memorial Stadium

Clairton-Glassport Bridge (sidewalk)

837

North State Street

CLAIRTON

885

Mendelssohn Avenue

Monongahela River

Montour Trail to Coraopolis, PA & Pittsburgh Intl. Airport

Clairton Connector
Part of U.S. Bicycle Route 50

Distance between the Great Allegheny Passage and the Montour Trail is approximately 4.5 miles (7.25 km)

A Project of the
Steel Valley Trail Council
and its Partners
www.steelvalleytrail.org

STEEL VALLEY TRAIL
C O U N C I L

© OpenStreetMap contributors, CC-BY-SA
www.openstreetmap.org
www.creativecommons.org

MILE 120.9 - Buena Vista: Buena Vista is a typical "patch" or coal company town. The small homes are placed closely together on the banks of the river and up the hillsides. Originally, four families lived in each house – one family per corner. You'll notice the multiple doors.

MILE 122.6 - Dravo Cemetery and Campground: Six miles from the Boston trailhead, you'll come to Dravo Cemetery. Dravo was once a small settlement with a Methodist Church, but only the cemetery remains today. The church caught fire from a spark from a passing train. Gravestones bear the names of nine Civil War veterans and one War of 1812 veteran. Boy Scouts constructed a campground here as a service project.

MILE 128.2 - Boston: Boston, or "Little Boston," as the locals call it, has trailhead parking and ballfields. This section of trail takes you past closed mills and other reminders of a more prosperous time.

MILE 129.2 - Dead Man's Hollow: This 400-acre preserve has several miles of hiking trails open for public use. It was likely named for the 1874 discovery by a group of boys of an unidentified man hanging from a tree in the hollow.

Jerome Street Bridge and McKeesport Marina.

Photo: Great Allegheny Passage Conservancy

MILE 132.5 - McKeesport: Located at the confluence of the Youghiogheny and Monongahela Rivers, McKeesport is also at the confluence of two trail systems. The GAP follows the "Mon" downriver to Pittsburgh; but, by crossing back over the Yough, cyclists can follow the Mon upriver along a 4.5 mile road route (see map, opposite) through Glassport and Clairton to access the 47-mile Montour Trail and a connector to the Pittsburgh International Airport. See pages 204-207 for a profile and town map.

Allegheny County Parks

alleghenyparks.com

9 BEAUTIFUL PARKS | 12,000+ ACRES | 180+ MILES OF TRAILS

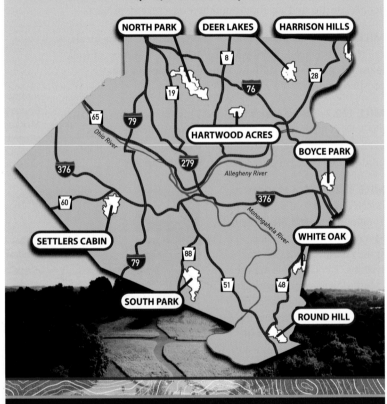

NORTH PARK · DEER LAKES · HARRISON HILLS · HARTWOOD ACRES · BOYCE PARK · SETTLERS CABIN · WHITE OAK · SOUTH PARK · ROUND HILL

MILE 134.1 - Riverton Bridge: This Union Railroad structure was decommissioned for railroad use in 2008 and rehabbed in record time for the Pittsburgh 250 anniversary celebration later that year. Built in 1890 by the Pencoyd Iron Works, which also built the Upper Steel Arch Bridge across Niagara Falls, it provided the rail connection to haul molten iron from the Duquesne Steel Works to the National Tube Works at McKeesport, and now connects these communities. A portion of the GAP is aligned with the Braddock Road, General Edward Braddock's path en route to Fort Duquesne and the site of his mortal wounding in 1755, during the Battle of the Monongahela.

MILE 135.3 - Duquesne: This was a steel town, with over 10,000 men working at U. S. Steel's Duquesne Works at its peak of operations. As you pass through here, you will see a few of its remaining buildings and the concrete wall that separated the plant from the railroad. The trail crosses, via two flyover bridges, busy railroad tracks hauling coal, freight and manufactured goods.

Riverton Bridge connects McKeesport to Duquesne.

Photo: Paul g Wiegman

The two flyover bridges are connected by trail built on a former U.S. Steel coke gas pipeline. Across the river, U.S. Steel's Edgar Thomson Works, the last steel plant in the valley, and the Braddock Lock and Dam, are clearly visible. Also in view are three roller coasters in Kennywood Park, which is a designated National Historic Landmark.

MILE 139.5 - The Pump House: This landmark was the locus of the 1892 Battle of Homestead, where locked-out and striking laborers clashed with Pinkerton agents hired by Carnegie Steel

Corporation's Henry Clay Frick. Today it is adjacent to a trail access area featuring restrooms (in the nearby Water Tower), bike racks, benches, and an outdoor labyrinth for reflection.

MILE 140.5 - Homestead: Along with its neighbors Munhall and West Homestead, this community is at the core of the region's transformation from steel manufacturing to service economies. The Eighth Avenue Historic District features new restaurants and craft breweries, and The Waterfront retail development has everything a trail traveler needs. See pages 208-211 for a profile and map.

MILE 145.2 - South Side: Here you can cross the Hot Metal Bridge toward downtown Pittsburgh and the GAP's western terminus, or stay on the South Side and explore one of the city's most vibrant neighborhoods. See pages 214-217 for a profile and map.

Built in 1901, the Hot Metal Bridge allowed for the movement of hot iron from the blast furnaces on the northern side of

the Monongahela River to the open hearths on the south side, and, in turn, the movement of steel ingots back to the rolling mills on the northern side. It opened for trail use in 2007 after a $10 million reconstruction project.

For over 140 years, the huge Jones & Laughlin Company (J&L) blast furnaces, open-hearth facilities, and neon J&L sign were landmarks

The Hot Metal Bridge.

Photo: Paul g Wiegman

along Second Avenue just outside downtown Pittsburgh. The steel mill was demolished in 1983, and in its place now stand the SouthSide Works and the Pittsburgh Technology Center.

MILE 148.8 - Downtown Pittsburgh: Once over the Hot Metal Bridge, the GAP follows the Eliza Furnace Trail – named for a series of J&L blast furnaces that occupied the banks of the Monongahela for over 100 years – to Grant Street in downtown

Pittsburgh. Cross Grant Street, and ride a dedicated bike/pedestrian chute to Smithfield Street. To your left is the Smithfield Street Bridge, an 1883 lenticular truss bridge named a National Historic Civic Engineering Landmark, and across the Monongahela River, the historic Pittsburgh and Lake Erie Railroad terminal, now the Grand Concourse Hotel.

Riding the GAP in Downtown Pittsburgh.

Photo: Great Allegheny Passage Conservancy

Take the new Monongahela Wharf Switchback down to the river, and follow the tree-lined promenade into the back of Point State Park and the GAP's western terminus. See pages 220–223 for details and a map.

MILE 148.8 - Point State Park: Bustling Point State Park is the outdoor recreation apex for downtown Pittsburgh, and its 36 acres are often enjoyed by noontime walkers and sunbathers during the week, and packed for festivals and concerts on weekends. It contains the footprints of long-gone Fort Duquesne and Fort Pitt, as well as the remaining Fort Pitt Block House, built in 1764 and the oldest authenticated structure west of the Allegheny Mountains. Stop in at the Fort Pitt Museum to learn about Pittsburgh's pivotal role during the French and Indian War.

At the tip of the park, where the Monongahela and the Allegheny join to form the Ohio River, you'll find a bronze medallion indicating the western terminus of the Great Allegheny Passage and the end of your journey.

SAMPLE ITINERARIES

From easy day trips to overnights to thru-trips. the best features of the Great Allegheny Passage and C&O Canal Towpath await you! Here are some of our favorite ideas.

TEN GREAT DAY TRIPS

1. REDSTONE RIDE (25.6 TOTAL MILES, C&O)

Park on the Maryland side of White's Ferry, once the site of a busy ferry service across the Potomac River. Head east on the C&O Canal Towapth to **Seneca Aqueduct** and **Riley's Lock**, the only place on the canal where a lock and aqueduct share a single structure. The famous Smithsonian Castle on the National Mall was built with red sandstone from the nearby quarry and transported by barge on the canal. A few hundred feet west of the aqueduct is a side trail to the ruins of the Seneca Quarry stone cutting mill. It's worth the short walk to explore these fascinating remains.

2. AQUEDUCT RUN (24.4 TOTAL MILES, C&O)

Start in **Brunswick, Md.** for lunch – the local favorite is spinach pie. Head east over the elliptical, three-arched **Catoctin Aqueduct** and the magnificent seven-arched **Monocacy Aqueduct**, both recently restored by the National Park Service. Stop at **Point of Rocks, Md.** to see the well-preserved Victorian train station. Notice how close the canal and the railroad are, and understand how this area got its name. Head back to Brunswick for ice cream.

3. JOHN BROWN'S RIDE (24.2 TOTAL MILES, C&O)

Park across the Potomac River from **Shepherdstown, W.Va.** and head east for a scenic 12.1 mile pedal to historic **Harpers Ferry, W.Va.** Carry your bicycle up the spiral staircase to cross the river into town. Explore the many historic buildings, museums and exhibits commemorating the Civil War. Ride back to Shepherdstown and enjoy dinner upon your return.

4. FOUR LOCKS TOUR (22.0 TOTAL MILES, C&O)

In **Williamsport, Md.**, park at the National Park Service Visitors Center at **Cushwa Basin**. Head west toward Dam 5, with its many interesting canal structures. Two miles further is the area known as **Four Locks**, built for the canal through Prathers Neck to eliminate a four mile bend in the river. Explore this historic area; you can even spend the night in a restored canal house. Have a snack at **McCoy's Ferry** recreation area before turning around.

5. FRUIT TO FORT (19.2 TOTAL MILES, C&O)

Start in Hancock, Md., once known as the fruit basket of the nation, because of the abundance of nearby orchards. Head east 9.6 miles to the beautifully restored Fort Frederick, originally built during the French and Indian War. Tour the fort before heading back, this time on the parallel, paved Western Maryland Rail Trail. Pies, produce and specialty foods make stopping for dinner in Hancock a must.

Four Locks
Photo: Steve Dean

Big Savage vista.

6. MOUNTAIN MARYLAND RIDE (41.0 TOTAL MILES, GAP)

Start in beautiful **Cumberland, Md.** and head toward cool **Frostburg, Md.**, 15.5 miles into the mountains. It's a slight and steady uphill grade with great views and a tight turn at Helmstetter's Curve. If you like, the Western Maryland Scenic Railroad can haul you and your bike up from Cumberland to Frostburg and you can arrive in style without breaking a sweat. Either way, we recommend lunch in Frostburg, a college town with a thriving arts scene and historic main street. Afterward, rejoin the trail and make the gentle climb to the **Mason & Dixon Line**, marked by a lovely commemorative park. Turn around for a 20.5-mile downhill cruise back to Cumberland.

7. RIDE THE DIVIDE (20.8 TOTAL MILES, GAP)

This ride features the most spectacular structures on the GAP and a chance to cross the **Eastern Continental Divide**. Start with breakfast in **Meyersdale, Pa.,** known for its maple syrup, and first head west to bike across the spectacular, 1,908 foot long, 101 feet high, **Salisbury Viaduct** that soars over the Casselman River. Turn around at the end of the viaduct and head back past your starting point. A few miles east of Meyersdale is the historic, relocated **Bollman Bridge**, the curving **Keystone Viaduct**, and seven small wooden bridges that cross over the meandering Flaugherty Run. Just past **Deal, Pa.**, the GAP reaches its high point at 2,392 feet above sea level. Go two more miles to pass through **Big Savage Tunnel**. Rest and take in the jaw-dropping vista (you can see into four states!) at the eastern end of the tunnel before you turn around and head back to Meyersdale.

8. THE ORIGINAL (20.6 TOTAL MILES, GAP)

This is the classic out-and-back GAP ride! Start in **Ohiopyle, Pa.** and head east on the first completed section of the GAP and through **Ohiopyle State Park**, famous for its whitewater rafting on the Youghiogheny River. The GAP meanders through the state's deepest gorge on your way to **Confluence, Pa.,** where there are many choices for lunch or dinner. Upon your return to Ohiopyle, be sure to check out the **Ohiopyle Low and High Bridges**, and take a short hike through **Ferncliff Peninsula Natural Area**, a National Natural Landmark.

9. CEDAR CREEK CIRCUIT (7.6 TOTAL MILES, GAP)

Park at **Cedar Creek Park**, and start with a pleasant nature walk through Cedar Creek Gorge. On the GAP, head west toward friendly **West Newton, Pa.** for a libation at a local distillery or brewery. Trail information and GAP merchandise is available at the visitors center in the reconstructed P&LE train station. While in West Newton, visit Simeral Square overlooking the Youghiogheny River, or tour the historic West Newton Cemetery.

10. PIPELINE COASTER (16.0 TOTAL MILES, GAP)

Explore this paved section of the GAP and feel the energy of the region's longtime steel manufacturing corridor. Start in **Homestead, Pa.** and head east, following the Monongahela River. Travel over the **Whitaker Flyover**, trace a former gas pipeline past Kennywood Amusement Park's famous roller coasters, and head over the **Port Perry Flyover**. Travel past a pipe fabricator in **Duquesne, Pa.,** near where General Edward

Recumbent tricyclist at the Eastern Continental Divide.

Photo: Great Allegheny Passage Conservancy

Braddock was once routed by French and Native American opponents, then cross the Riverton Bridge for a look into McKeesport. Head back and enjoy any of the many dining options when you return.

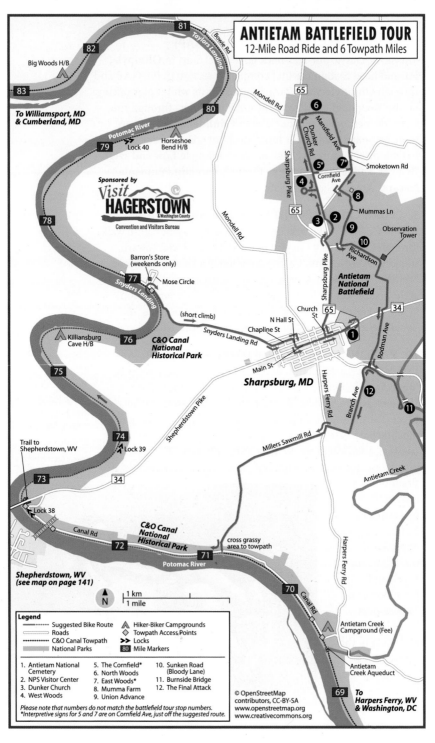

ANTIETAM BATTLEFIELD TOUR
12-Mile Road Ride and 6 Towpath Miles

Taylors Landing
Bowie Rd
Big Woods H/B
81
82
83
To Williamsport, MD & Cumberland, MD
Potomac River
79 Lock 40
Horseshoe Bend H/B
80
Mondell Rd
65
6
Mansfield Ave
Dunker Church Rd
Sharpsburg Pike
Mondell Rd

Sponsored by
Visit HAGERSTOWN
& Washington County
Convention and Visitors Bureau

78

5 7
Cornfield Ave
Smoketown Rd
4
65
8
Mummas Ln
3 2
9
Observation Tower
10
Richardson Ave

Barron's Store (weekends only)
Mose Circle
77
Snyders Landing
Antietam National Battlefield

(short climb)
N Hall St
Chapline St
Church St
65
34
Killiansburg Cave H/B
76
C&O Canal National Historical Park
Snyders Landing Rd
1
Rodman Ave
75
Sharpsburg, MD
Main St
Harpers Ferry Rd
Branch Ave
12
11
Shepherdstown Pike
74 Lock 39
34
Millers Sawmill Rd
Antietam Creek

Trail to Shepherdstown, WV
73 Lock 38
Canal Rd
72
C&O Canal National Historical Park
cross grassy area to towpath
71
Potomac River
Harpers Ferry Rd

Shepherdstown, WV (see map on page 141)
70
Canal Rd

N
1 km
1 mile

Antietam Creek Campground (Fee)

69 *To Harpers Ferry, WV & Washington, DC*

Antietam Creek Aqueduct

© OpenStreetMap contributors, CC-BY-SA
www.openstreetmap.org
www.creativecommons.org

Legend
- .... Suggested Bike Route
- —— Roads
- .... C&O Canal Towpath
- National Parks
- ⛺ Hiker-Biker Campgrounds
- ◇ Towpath Access Points
- ➤➤ Locks
- 80 Mile Markers

1. Antietam National Cemetery
2. NPS Visitor Center
3. Dunker Church
4. West Woods
5. The Cornfield*
6. North Woods
7. East Woods*
8. Mumma Farm
9. Union Advance
10. Sunken Road (Bloody Lane)
11. Burnside Bridge
12. The Final Attack

Please note that numbers do not match the battlefield tour stop numbers.
*Interpretive signs for 5 and 7 are on Cornfield Ave, just off the suggested route.

SIX AMAZING WEEKEND TRIPS

TRIP 1: CIVIL WAR CYCLE (C&O)

DAY	START/END	TURN AROUND	MILEAGE
1	Brunswick, Md.	Whites Ferry	39.0
2	Brunswick, Md.	Shepherdstown, W.Va	35.6

Set up base camp in historic **Frederick, Md.**, where you'll find many lodging and dining options for this weekend trip. Monocacy National Battlefield is five miles away and the National Museum of Civil War Medicine is right in town.

On your first day, drive 15 miles to **Brunswick, Md.** where you'll find parking near the railroad station. Head east on the C&O toward the magnificent **Monocacy Aqueduct**, which was often under Confederate attack. Continue to Whites Ferry to gaze at where the last operating ferry across the Potomac River finally discontinued service in 2020. Eat lunch, then ride back to your car.

On day two, start again in Brunswick, but head west on the C&O Can Towpath instead. Across from Harpers Ferry, climb the spiral steps and cross the river to tour **Harpers Ferry National Historical Park** where John Brown led his ill-fated raid on a federal armory in his quest to abolish slavery. Continue on to **Shepherdstown, W.Va.** for lunch at one of the many restaurants on German Street. If you've got the energy, add an 18-mile on-road loop to the town of **Sharpsburg, Md.** (see map on opposite page) to visit **Antietam National Battlefield**,

From Harper's Weekly, *1861: Monocacy Aqueduct.*

site of the bloodiest one-day battle in American history. The climb is 2.5 percent for the first mile, then levels to rolling country roads. Then make your way 17.8 miles back to Brunswick.

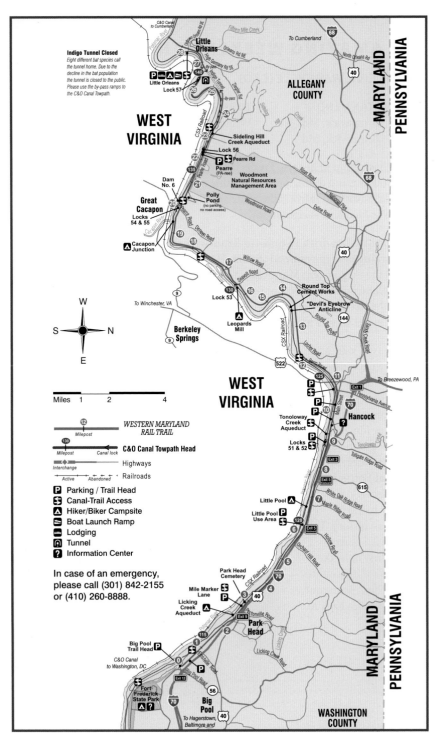

Indigo Tunnel Closed
Eight different bat species call the tunnel home. Due to the decline in the bat population the tunnel is closed to the public. Please use the by-pass ramps to the C&O Canal Towpath.

WEST VIRGINIA

ALLEGANY COUNTY

Little Orleans

Lock 57

Sideling Hill Creek Aqueduct

Lock 56

Pearre Rd
Pearre (PA-ree)

Woodmont Natural Resources Management Area

Dam No. 6

Polly Pond
(no parking, no road access)

Great Cacapon
Locks 54 & 55

Cacapon Junction

Willow Road

Lock 53

Round Top Cement Works
"Devil's Eyebrow" Anticline

Leopards Mill

To Winchester, VA

Berkeley Springs

WEST VIRGINIA

To Breezewood, PA

Tonoloway Creek Aqueduct

Hancock

Locks 51 & 52

Little Pool

Little Pool Use Area

Park Head Cemetery

Mile Marker Lane

Licking Creek Aqueduct

Park Head

Big Pool Trail Head

C&O Canal to Washington, DC

Fort Frederick State Park

Big Pool

To Hagerstown, Baltimore and

WASHINGTON COUNTY

In case of an emergency, please call (301) 842-2155 or (410) 260-8888.

W N S E

Miles 1 2 4

12 Milepost — WESTERN MARYLAND RAIL TRAIL

130 Milepost Canal lock — C&O Canal Towpath Head

Interchange — Highways

Active Abandoned — Railroads

P Parking / Trail Head
S Canal-Trail Access
▲ Hiker/Biker Campsite
🚢 Boat Launch Ramp
🛏 Lodging
🏛 Tunnel
? Information Center

MARYLAND

PENNSYLVANIA

TRIP 2: HANCOCK BOWTIE (C&O)

DAY	START/END	TURN AROUND	MILEAGE
1	Hancock, Md.	Sideling Hill Creek	25.0
2	Hancock, Md.	Fort Frederick	19.2

This round trip takes the shape of a bow tie beginning and ending in Hancock. The first day, head west on the C&O from **Hancock, Md.** along the Potomac River, passing the remnants of the lime kilns of the **Round Top Cement Mill**. At Sideling Hill Creek, 12.5 miles west, there is a crossover path to the paved Western Maryland Rail Trail (see map on opposite page) for a smooth ride back. The next day, pack a lunch from a Hancock eatery and head east on the C&O, passing "Big Pool,"

Photo: Great Allegheny Passage Conservancy

a wide section of the canal once convenient for turning boats around. Visit Fort Frederick State Park, an outpost built to protect the interests of British colonialists against the French and their Native American allies. The grounds are a perfect place for a walking tour. Take the Western Maryland Rail Trail back to Hancock.

TRIP 3: BYOB WEEKEND IN HARPERS FERRY (C&O)

DAY	START/END	TURN AROUND	MILEAGE
1	Harpers Ferry, W.Va.	Shepherdstown, W.Va.	24.2
2	Harpers Ferry, W.Va.	Brunswick, Md.	11.4

Take Amtrak to historic **Harpers Ferry, W.Va.**, from wherever you can catch the Capitol Limited (see page 36) When you are ready to start your day one ride, cross the Potomac River on the bike/ped bridge, make your way down the spiral steps to the C&O Canal Towpath, and head west to **Shepherdstown, W.Va.**, a college town with lots of shops, historic sites, and restaurants. Ride back to your lodging in Harpers Ferry.

On day two, walk the stone stairs that carry the Appalachian Trail to Jefferson Rock and enjoy the morning sun. Ride out to **Brunswick, Md.** for lunch and a tour of town. Head back to Harpers Ferry and walk **Harpers Ferry National Historical Park** in the afternoon, exploring Civil War battlefields or the many historic buildings in Harpers Ferry or neighboring Bolivar.

TRIP 4: OVER THE RIVER AND THROUGH THE WOODS (GAP)

DAY	START	END/LODGING	MILEAGE
1	Connellsville, Pa.	Rockwood, Pa.	45.0
2	Rockwood, Pa.	Cumberland, Md.	43.8

Starting in **Connellsville, Pa.**, and heading to **Cumberland, Md.**, you'll cover 88.8 miles over two days. Your first 27.2 will be through the thick forest canopies of **Ohiopyle State Park**, while crossing high above the bubbling Youghiogheny River twice. Have lunch at a cafe in **Confluence, Pa.**, and then cross the Casselman River twice on your way out of town. Two more river crossings near the **Pinkerton Tunnel**, and you finish in **Rockwood, Pa.**, where there are B&B's very close to the trail. Your second day features a fifth river crossing using the soaring **Salisbury Viaduct**, a visit to **Meyersdale, Pa.**, and then eight crossings of Flaughtery Run as you head to the **Mason & Dixon Line**. In Maryland, you'll catch valley vistas on the 20.5 miles to Cumberland, where dinner and an evening Amtrak ride back to Connellsville await.

TRIP 5: MINES AND MANSIONS (GAP)

DAY	START	END/LODGING	MILEAGE
1	Confluence, Pa.	Connellsville, Pa.	27.2
2	Connellsville, Pa.	West Newton, Pa.	25.3

This 52.5-mile, two-day ride takes you from **Confluence, Pa.** – visit the town square, or gaze over Youghiogheny Lake from atop the nearby dam – to **West Newton, Pa.** Arrange for a shuttle back. Ride west along the Youghiogheny River and trace the deep gorges it cut through the ridges of the Allegheny Mountains. In 10.3 miles, stop at **Ohiopyle, Pa.**, and take a shuttle up to **Fallingwater**, Frank Lloyd Wright's legendary cantilevered private retreat. (Get tickets for both in advance.) Afterward, pick up a picnic lunch. Then continue west through 16.9 more miles of gorgeous Ohiopyle State Park, and into **Connellsville, Pa.** for lodging at one of the city's many turn-of-last century mansions.

When morning breaks, head west again. After 4.1 miles, you'll wind past the Connellsville Coke Ovens, where coal was baked into high-quality fuel for the region's steel industry. Shortly thereafter, detour across the river to **Dawson**, a tiny hamlet featuring amazing gingerbread-laden homes once occupied by coke barons and baronesses. Return to the GAP and past several shuttered coal mines, one of which is being transformed into an artistic memorial to 239 miners killed in the Darr Mine disaster. When you get to West Newton, grab dinner and a local drink, and wait for your shuttle back to Confluence.

TRIP 6: STEEL VALLEY VOLLEY (GAP)

DAY	START	END/LODGING	MILEAGE
1	West Newton, Pa.	Pittsburgh's South Side	31.1
2	Pittsburgh's South Side	West Newton, Pa.	31.1

Launch your ride in **West Newton, Pa.** Pack a lunch from one of West Newton's cafes or restaurants, and head west for an overnight on Pittsburgh's artsy **South Side.** En route, stop at the historic **Dravo Cemetery** adjacent to the hiker-biker campground along the **Youghiogheny River,** and find the Civil War-era tombstones. The Methodist church once here burned twice, allegedly by fires started by sparks from trains rushing by. In **Boston, Pa.,** stop at the preserved Pittsburgh & Lake Erie boxcar. Boston was named for Boston, Massachusetts, and the granite mile markers along the GAP were cut from stone collected from the Longfellow Bridge there.

In **McKeesport,** the GAP winds past the McKeesport Marina and turns to parallel the mighty **Monongahela River.** Watch for signs commemorating British General Edward Braddock's failed path toward Fort Duquesne in 1755. Climb the **Port Perry Flyover** and ride a stretch of the GAP not built on old railroads, but former gas lines, underneath the soaring coasters of Kennywood Park to the **Whitaker Flyover.** Once in **Homestead, Pa.,** pause at the Pump House, the remaining structure from the deadly 1892 Homestead Steel Strike. Then, on Pittsburgh's South Side, park your bike and explore the neighborhood's public murals, ethnic restaurants, shot-and-a-beer bars. Stay overnight at a guest house or hotel.

The next morning, catch the sunrise at **Point State Park,** breakfast at a Pittsburgh diner, the exhibits at the **Fort Pitt Museum,** and then head back to West Newton for dinner and a craft brew.

Bicyclists riding up the Whitaker Flyover. Photo: Great Allegheny Passage Conservancy

FOUR THRU-TRIPS

1. PEDAL THE PASSAGE (FOUR DAYS, THREE NIGHTS)

This 148.8-mile itinerary takes you end-to-end on the Great Allegheny Passage from **Pittsburgh** to **Cumberland, Md.** It's oriented to give you the benefit of tailwinds and the fun of the 23.7-mile downhill coast into Cumberland at the end. With daily distances of 30-40 miles, this schedule gives you time for leisurely lunch breaks, exploring, and picture-taking. It has the benefit of overnight lodging options in guesthouses or B&B's each night.

DAY	START	END/LODGING	DISTANCE
1	Downtown Pittsburgh	West Newton, Pa.	34.7 miles
2	West Newton, Pa.	Ohiopyle, Pa.	42.2 miles
3	Ohiopyle, Pa.	Meyersdale, Pa.	40.0 miles
4	Meyersdale, Pa.	Cumberland, Md.	31.9 miles

Amtrak's bicycle service makes this trip easy to pull off. You can leave your vehicle at either end and take the Capitol Limited in the opposite direction. We've suggested starting in Pittsburgh, but you can start in Cumberland if you please. Whichever you choose, be sure to explore **Canal Place** near Mile Zero in Cumberland, and **Point State Park** in Pittsburgh, home of the GAP's western terminus. Both Cumberland and Pittsburgh feature great restaurants, breweries, distilleries, special events, river views, paddling, museums, art galleries, and all kinds of fun to celebrate the end of your trip.

GAP Mile Zero at Canal Place, Cumberland.
Photo: Eric Randall

2. THE RIDE OF YOUR LIFE (SIX DAYS, FIVE NIGHTS)

This 333.3-mile **Pittsburgh**-to-**Washington, D.C.** trip is the classic bucket list adventure, with 50-60 mile days. Whether you carry your own gear or hire a shuttle service, this itinerary is designed for staying in bed and breakfasts, inns, hotels, or guesthouses, and allows you leisurely lunches in trail towns, with plenty of time in the evenings to relax and recuperate. This trip is certainly reversible from east to west if you so choose. Reserve a ticket and bike slot on Amtrak's Capitol Limited for a convenient return trip.

DAY	START	END/LODGING	DISTANCE
1	Downtown Pittsburgh	Connellsville, Pa.	60.0 miles
2	Connellsville, Pa.	Rockwood, Pa.	45.0 miles
3	Rockwood, Pa.	Cumberland, Md.	43.8 miles
4	Cumberland Md.	Hancock, Md.	60.4 miles
5	Hancock, Md.	Harpers Ferry, W.Va.	63.4 miles
6	Harpers Ferry, W.Va.	Washington, D.C.	60.7 miles

Bicyclists in an old railroad cut near Frostburg.
Photo: Doug Reigner

3. CAMPING TREK (NINE DAYS, EIGHT NIGHTS)

Ready to slow-roll with all your gear, independent and free? Here's one variant of a self-supported trip that takes advantage of the many hiker-biker campgrounds along the C&O Canal Towpath and commercial campgrounds along

Photo: Paul g Wiegman

the GAP. You can do it in a week plus two adjacent weekends. We suggest starting in **Washington, D.C.** to tackle the bumpier towpath first. Use Amtrak or a shuttle service for your return trip. For other options, check out our longer list of campgrounds on pages 38 and 39.

DAY	START	END/CAMPGROUND	DISTANCE
1	Washington, D.C.	Chisel Branch Hiker-Biker	30.5 miles
2	Chisel Branch Hiker-Biker	Huckleberry Hill Hiker-Biker	32.4 miles
3	Huckleberry Hill Hiker-Biker	Jordan Junction Hiker-Biker	38.3 miles
4	Jordan Junction Hiker-Biker	Indigo Neck Hiker-Biker	38.0 miles
5	Indigo Neck Hiker-Biker	Evitts Creek Hiker-Biker	40.9 miles
6	Evitt's Creek Hiker-Biker	Maple Festival Park Primitive Camping	36.3 miles
7	Maple Festival Park Primitive Camping	Youghiogheny River Dam Outflow	29.5 miles
8	Youghiogheny River Dam Outflow	Cedar Creek Park Hiker-Biker	48.8 miles
9	Cedar Creek Park Hiker-Biker	Downtown Pittsburgh	38.6 miles

4. BOTH TRAILS, EASILY (FOUR THREE-DAY WEEKENDS)

If you can't arrange to take a week or so for the trip, you can still ride both the GAP and C&O (all 333.3 miles!) over four long weekends. Here's one way to do it, with most days in the 25- to 35-mile range. Get picked up or rent one-way to return to your starting spot. This itinerary is largely amenable to lodging in nearby trail towns. It's best for bicyclists, but hikers or ultramarathoners might find it doable with adequate training and perhaps a shuttle service to handle gear.

Ride One: Pittsburgh to Confluence, Pa. (GAP)

DAY	START	END/LODGING	DISTANCE
1	Downtown Pittsburgh	West Newton, Pa.	34.7 miles
2	West Newton, Pa.	Connellsvillle, Pa.	25.3 miles
3	Connellsville, Pa.	Confluence, Pa.	27.2 miles

Ride Two: Confluence, Pa. to the Paw Paw Tunnel (GAP/C&O)

DAY	START	END/LODGING	DISTANCE
1	Confluence, Pa.	Meyersdale, Pa.	29.7 miles
2	Meyersdale, Pa.	Cumberland, Md.	31.9 miles
3	Cumberland, Md.	Paw Paw Tunnel (Md.)	28.4 miles

Ride Three: Paw Paw Tunnel to Shepherdstown, W.Va. (C&O)

DAY	START	END/LODGING	DISTANCE
1	Paw Paw Tunnel (Md.)	Hancock, Md.	32.0 miles
2	Hancock, Md.	Williamsport, Md.	24.7 miles
3	Williamsport, Md.	Shepherdstown, W.Va.	26.6 miles

Ride Four: Shepherdstown, W.Va. to Washington, D.C. (C&O)

DAY	START	END/LODGING	DISTANCE
1	Shepherdstown, W.Va.	Harpers Ferry, W.Va	12.1 miles
2	Harpers Ferry, W.Va.	Brunswick, Md.	5.7 miles
3	Brunswick, Md.	Washington, D.C.	55.0 miles

The C&O Canal and Towpath in Washington, D.C.'s Georgetown neighborhood.

Photo: Bob Rives / Georgetown Business Improvement District

GEORGETOWN

WASHINGTON D.C.

ELEVATION 15 FEET • C&O 0.0

Washington, D.C.'s Georgetown neighborhood is a historic port town that predates the establishment of the federal district itself. It is home to an eclectic mix of art galleries, cafés, clothiers, boutiques, luxury hotels, fine restaurants, bookstores, foreign embassies, and a world-class university. Lively **M Street** boasts a vibrant nightlife, and the **Georgetown Waterfront Park** features some of the most picturesque kayaking, running, and bicycling backdrops the city has to offer. The **Francis Scott Key Memorial** gathers tourists at a brownstone brick plaza covered by a limestone pergola, draped in wisteria. Many of the city's finest historic brick and frame row houses line quiet side streets.

The neighborhood showcases famous federalist architecture and 19th century mansions. The **Old Stone House**, dating to 1765, is the oldest standing building in the city. The **Dumbarton House**, erected in 1799, contains rotating exhibits of household furnishings, art, and décor from the federalist period. And **Tudor Place**, built by Martha Washington's granddaughter in 1816, is home to the extensive Mt. Vernon collection.

The C&O Canal Towpath snakes through Georgetown almost unnoticed, yet nearly two hundred years ago, the canal was the pivotal launching point for executing George Washington's vision to open up the western lands via a navigable alternative to the **Potomac River**. For much of the 19th century, Georgetown was a busy commercial hub for transferring imports and exports, including tobacco, sugar, flour, and coal.

This section of the C&O Canal is currently undergoing a multi-year revitalization and reactivation, including extensive work to rebuild Lock 3 and rejuvenate Lock 4, led by **Georgetown Heritage** and the **National Park Service**, with support from the **Georgetown Business Improvement District**.

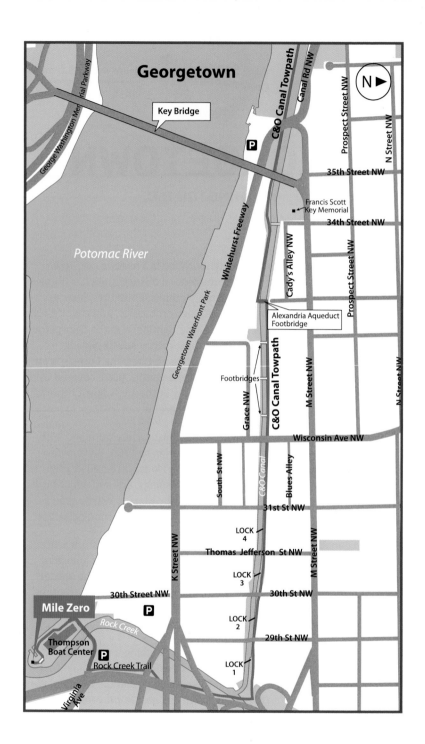

Georgetown

Key Bridge

C&O Canal Towpath

Canal Rd NW

Prospect Street NW

N Street NW

35th Street NW

Francis Scott
Key Memorial

34th Street NW

Potomac River

Whitehurst Freeway

Cady's Alley NW

Prospect Street NW

Alexandria Aqueduct
Footbridge

Georgetown Waterfront Park

Footbridges

Grace NW

C&O Canal Towpath

M Street NW

N Street NW

Wisconsin Ave NW

South St NW

C&O Canal

Blues Alley

31st St NW

LOCK 4

Thomas Jefferson St NW

M Street NW

K Street NW

LOCK 3

30th Street NW

30th St NW

Mile Zero

Rock Creek

LOCK 2

29th St NW

Thompson
Boat Center

Rock Creek Trail

LOCK 1

Virginia Ave

FINDING MILE ZERO OF THE C&O CANAL TOWPATH

Mile Zero of the C&O Canal Towpath, in Washington D.C.'s Georgetown neighborhood, is marked by a modest granite monument behind Thompson Boat Center, where Rock Creek empties into the Potomac River. If you're at the Mile Zero marker and are headed to Pittsburgh, walk your bike around Thompson Boat Center and cross the narrow bridge over Rock Creek. Turn left onto Rock Creek Trail. Cross over the exit ramp for the Whitehurst Freeway (there's a crosswalk), pass underneath K Street, and then cross over the entrance ramp (another crosswalk). Cross Rock Creek again, and then turn left onto the C&O Canal Towpath. The towpath parallels the canal, crossing at the Alexandria Aqueduct footbridge and heads toward Cumberland.

If you are traveling into Washington D.C.'s Georgetown neighborhood on the C&O Canal Towpath from Cumberland, follow the towpath until it ends at Rock Creek Trail. Turn right. Follow Rock Creek Trail, crossing over Rock Creek and then the entrance ramp to the Whitehurst Freeway (there's a crosswalk). Pass underneath K Street, and cross over the exit ramp (another crosswalk). Turn right toward Thompson Boat Center (there are signs), crossing over Rock Creek again. Walk your bike to the back of Thompson Boat Center to find the Mile Zero Marker.

Photo: Taylor Nielson, Wilderness Voyageurs

A 45-foot mosaic on East Potomac Street features a likeness of Dr. Arlington Horine, of Horine's Drug Store and Soda Fountain Shop.

Barbara Badstibner, with permission from Brunswick Main Street

BRUNSWICK

FREDERICK COUNTY, MARYLAND

ELEVATION 242 FEET • C&O 55.0

Founded as the village of Berlin, both the **B&O Railroad** and the C&O Canal arrived here in 1834. For the first fifty years, the Canal had a greater impact on the town's economy. In 1890 the town incorporated as Brunswick and became a major hub for the railroad, which built a six-mile long railyard along the Potomac and boosted the population to over 5,000.

Today, Brunswick is a stop on the MARC commuter rail station serving Washington, D.C. The restored Queen Anne style station has been on its present site since 1907. Its main street features an outfitter, a bike shop, a craft brewery, a cafe, an ice creamery, and many other retail options. A nearby campground is a great option for lodging.

On West Potomac Street is the **Brunswick Heritage Museum** and National Park Service Visitor Center filled with exhibits about the canal, railroad, and community; it is open limited hours Thursdays, Fridays, Saturdays, and Sundays.

Celebrate the small-but-mighty in Frederick County's littlest city on **Small City Saturdays**. From bonfires to baseball, the second Saturday of the month in Brunswick offers activities and attractions that the whole family will enjoy! Downtown also hosts regional festivals like **Bike to Work Day Pitstop** in May, the **Throwback on the Towpath** in August, and **Annual Railroad Days in October.**

For more information, go to **www.brunswickmainstreet.org.**

easy access from trail to town

Use your smart phone to scan the
QR code for more information
about visiting Brunswick, MD.

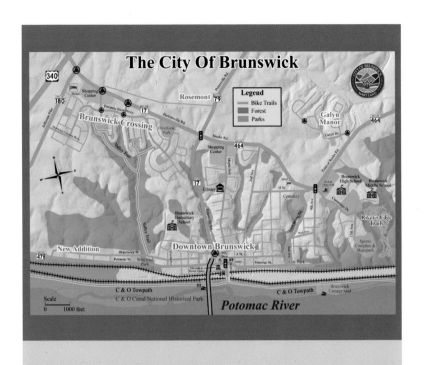

The City Of Brunswick

Legend
- Bike Trails
- Forest
- Parks

Rosemont

Galyn Manor

Brunswick Crossing

Brunswick High School

Brunswick Middle School

River's Edge Trails

Brunswick Elementary School

New Addition

Downtown Brunswick

Sports Complex & Skatepark

C & O Towpath

C & O Canal National Historical Park

C & O Towpath

Brunswick Campground

Scale
0 — 1000 feet

Potomac River

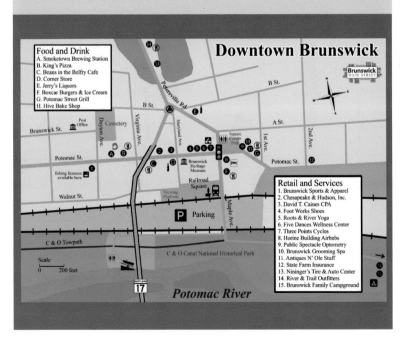

Downtown Brunswick

Food and Drink
A. Smoketown Brewing Station
B. King's Pizza
C. Beans in the Belfry Cafe
D. Corner Store
E. Jerry's Liquors
F. Boxcar Burgers & Ice Cream
G. Potomac Street Grill
H. Hive Bake Shop

Brunswick MAIN STREET

Post Office

Cemetery

Brunswick St.

Potomac St.

fishing licences available here

Walnut St.

Brunswick Heritage Museum

Railroad Square

Viewing Platform

P Parking

C & O Towpath

Scale
0 — 200 feet

Retail and Services
1. Brunswick Sports & Apparel
2. Chesapeake & Hudson, Inc.
3. David T. Caines CPA
4. Foot Works Shoes
5. Roots & River Yoga
6. Five Dances Wellness Center
7. Three Points Cycles
8. Horine Building Airbnbs
9. Public Spectacle Optometry
10. Brunswick Grooming Spa
11. Antiques N' Ole Stuff
12. State Farm Insurance
13. Nininger's Tire & Auto Center
14. River & Trail Outfitters
15. Brunswick Family Campground

C & O Canal National Historical Park

Potomac River

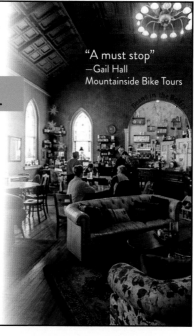
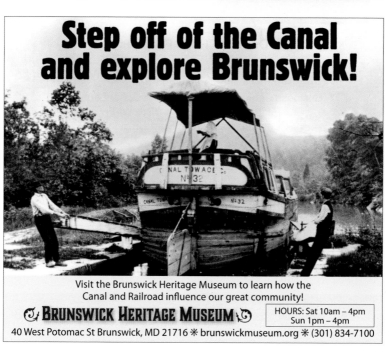

Corner Store

Corner Store is your ultimate refueling & resupply stop. Beer, wine, soft drinks, snacks plus travel-sized first-aid and personal care items, two minutes from the trail.

102 W Potomac St,
Brunswick, MD 21716
301-658-4593

Three Points Cycles

New bike sales, repairs, and bike packing gear. Find quotes for common repairs on our website. For after-hours emergencies, message us through Facebook.

5 W Potomac Street
Brunswick, MD 21716
301-834-7199
threepointcycles.com

DAVID T. CAINES, CPA

With over 25 years of experience, our team has the expertise to ensure professional, personable, accurate, and high-quality service. Tax preparation, accounting, financial analysis, tax planning, business development and formation, as well as bookkeeping payroll.

101 W. Potomac St, Brunswick, MD
301-834-7176
cainescpa.com

Blue-COLLAR Craft

Smoketown Brewing

Just steps off mile marker 55 on the C&O Canal and Potomac River. Serving Maryland award winning craft beer. Open Wed. through Sun. 24 beers always on tap. Indoor and outdoor seating, music, food. Bike racks across the street.

233 W. Potomac Street
Brunswick, MD 21716
301-834-4828
smoketownbrewing.com

Harpers Ferry rooflines in autumn mist.

Photo: Don Burgess

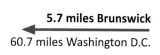

HARPERS FERRY BOLIVAR

JEFFERSON COUNTY, WEST VIRGINIA

ELEVATION 250 FEET • C&O 60.7

The towns sit at the confluence of the Potomac and Shenandoah Rivers where the states of Maryland, Virginia, and West Virginia meet.

The lower part of Harpers Ferry has been preserved because of its important place in United States history. **Harpers Ferry National Historical Park** focuses on its extensive Civil War history, best known for **John Brown's Raid** on the Federal Armory in 1859, sparking the start of the Civil War.

Today, **Harpers Ferry Historic District** shows off many restored nineteenth century buildings now converted into museums honoring the town's history. The red-sandstone-trimmed St. Peter's Catholic Church sits high above on a prominent knob and travelers can easily find restaurants, guesthouses, B&B's, outfitters, and dozens of unique retail shops. Amtrak's Capitol Limited stops here, and picnic spots with great views are abundant.

For outdoor fun, you can rent rafts and tubes for whitewater rafting or lazy river float trips. Climb the stone steps to **Jefferson Rock** for a panoramic view, praised by Thomas Jefferson as "perhaps one of the most stupendous scenes in Nature." A popular hike from the towpath is the 4.5 mile climb up and down **Maryland Heights**. With a spectacular view of Harpers Ferry from the main overlook, this shorter circuit is a favorite for many. The trailhead is located near C&O mile 61.

Lovely Bolivar, an adjacent residential community, contains several B&B's, a library, restaurants, a summer farmers market, and a café.

For a closer look, visit **www.discoveritallwv.com**.

Experience
HARPERS FERRY / BOLIVAR

Creating Memories to Last a Lifetime!

SHOP

16	Blue Point Jewelry	571-527-8978
38	Gilded Flea	304-268-0763
53	H.B. Snallygaster General Store & Café	ⓕ @snally1920
3	Harpers Ferry Outfitters	304-535-2087
10	Harpers Ferry Park Association Bookshop	304-535-6881
13	The Hodge Podge	304-535-6917
27	Nature's Health & Body	772-228-HEMP
19	Magpie Pottery	757-376-1748
18	Mary Adams Accessories	304-535-2411
25	The Country Store at the Towns' Inn	304-932-0677 or 304-702-1872 (mobile)
6	Tenfold Fair Trade Collection	304-579-8525
18	Tessoterica	304-535-8248
11	True Treats Historic Candy	304-461-4714
11	The Village Shop at Harpers Ferry	304-535-8333
23	The Vintage Lady	304-535-1313
52	Washington Street Studios	240-586-1126
67	White Fly Outfitters	304-876-8030

EAT

2	A La Mode Cafe	540-514-6255
5	Almost Heaven Pub & Grill	304-535-8710
48	Anvil Restaurant	304-535-2582
49	The Barn—Harpers Ferry Pub & Event Venue	855-935-2276
20	Battle Grounds Bakery & Coffee	304-535-8583
37	Bolivar Bread	703-980-0737
12	Cannonball Deli	304-535-1762
15	Coach House Grill 'n Bar	540-514-6255
1	Coffee Mill	540-514-6255
62	Country Café	304-535-2327
4	Creamy Creations	304-535-8710
53	H.B. Snallygaster General Store & Café	ⓕ @snally1920
70	Harpers Ferry Ice Cream Shoppe	304-535-6305
54	Kelley Farm Kitchen	304-535-9976
26	Mountain House Café	304-932-0677 or 304-702-1872 (mobile)
25	Old Fireman's BBQ & Catering Company	304-535-8503
21	The Rabbit Hole	304-535-8818
24	Isabella's Pizza & Subs	304-535-8769
70	White Horse Tavern	304-535-6314

STAY

32	Angler's Inn B&B	304-535-1239
70	Clarion Inn Harpers Ferry-Charles Town	304-535-6302
33	Harpers Ferry Guest House & Carrot Top Cottage	304-804-3204
66	Harpers Ferry KOA	304-535-6895
61	Harpers Ferry Tails Pet Sitting	301-742-9681 or 304-867-9757
44	Harpers Ferry Vacation Rentals	877-468-4236
43	The Jackson Rose B&B	304-535-1528
50	La Soledad Lavender Farm and Guesthouse	317-270-4133
28	Ledge House B&B	877-468-4236
47	The Light Horse Inn	877-468-4236
30	Lily Garden B&B	304-535-2657
41	Marbrun House Airbnb	703-967-2226
50	Marie's Inn Airbnb	703-407-0183
22	Mountainside Lodge	240-372-0499
42	Quality Inn Harpers Ferry	304-535-6391
79	River & Trail Outfitters & Brunswick Family Campground	301-834-9950
71	River Riders Vacation Rentals & Campground	304-535-2663
45	Rockhaven B&B	304-535-8235
14	Stonehouse B&B	304-460-9550
26	The Town's Inn	304-932-0677 or 304-702-1872 (mobile)
29	Trouvaille House	airbnb.com/rooms/50135945
35	Two Rivers Guesthouse	703-727-2907

PLAY

25	American Health & Heritage Adventure Academy	304-932-0677
31	Appalachian Trail Visitor Center	304-535-6331
49	The Barn of Harpers Ferry	855-935-BARN
9	Ghost Tours of Harpers Ferry	304-725-8019
6	C&O Canal National Historical Park	
81	Harpers Ferry Adventure Center	540-668-9007
8	Harpers Ferry Bikes	304-804-3204
10	Harpers Ferry Certified Guide Tours	304-535-6881
65	Harpers Ferry National Historical Park	304-535-6029
3	Harpers Ferry Outfitters Bike & Hike	304-535-2087
82	Harpers Ferry Toy Train Museum	304-535-2521
63	Jefferson County Visitor Center	304-535-2627
17	John Brown Wax Museum	304-535-6342

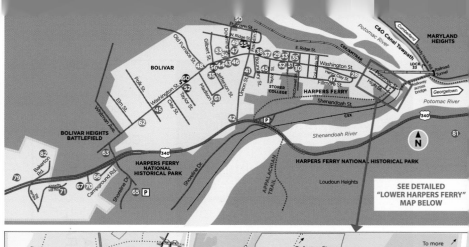

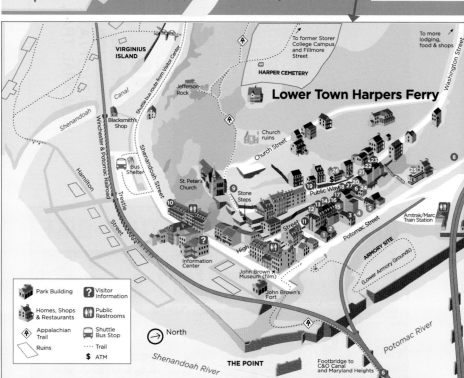

Lower Town Harpers Ferry

Legend	
Park Building	Visitor Information
Homes, Shops & Restaurants	Public Restrooms
Appalachian Trail	Shuttle Bus Stop
Ruins	Trail
	$ ATM

9 O' Be Joyful Tours & Concerts 732-801-0381

79 River & Trail Outfitters
    & Brunswick Family Campground 301-834-9950

71 River Riders Family Adventure Resort ... 304-535-2663

67 White Fly Outfitters 304-876-8030

45 Rations Spaceport Virtual   rationsspaceport.com
    Reality & Escape Adventures

JEFFERSON
COUNTY
CONVENTION & VISITORS BUREAU

SERVICES

31 Appalachian Trail Visitor Center 304-535-6331

26 ATM

55 BB&T ATM

60 BCT - ATM 304-535-6336
    Bank of Charles Town

65 Harpers Ferry National Historical 304-535-6029
    Park Visitors Center

61 Harpers Ferry Tails Pet Sitting 301-742-9681
                                        or 304-867-9757

63 Jefferson County Convention & 304-535-2627
    Visitor Bureau Welcome Center

Quality Inn

Escape to Harpers Ferry with a free hot breakfast, fresh waffles, premium free Wifi, flat screen HDTV, premium movies, microwave/fridge, bike wash and fitness center.

877-4-CHOICE (877-424-6423)
304-535-6391
choicehotels.com/hotel/WV406
100 yards to Appalachian Trail
One mile to C&O Canal

Outfitters at Harpers Ferry

We are an outfitter store for hiking and biking, selling a wide range of products for the hiker, the cyclist, & adventure traveler. Trail food resupply, bike parts, Harpers Ferry mercantile.

161 Potomac St. Harpers Ferry WV
(304) 535-2087
outfitter1996@yahoo.com
Find us on Facebook

The Town's Inn

Enjoy year-round dining, shopping, & lodging at the Town's Inn, which is located just steps from the C&O Towpath & Appalachian Trail in the middle of the Harpers Ferry historical market district.

175 & 179 High St. Harper's Ferry
304.932.0677   mobile 304.702.1872
KaranTownsend@gmail.com
www.TheTownsInn.com

Battle Grounds

Breakfast & lunch sandwiches on our fresh baked bread. Offering pastries, espresso, specialty coffees, smoothies, and much more. Open year round, indoor/outdoor seating.

304-535-8583
180 High Street
Harper's Ferry, WV 25425
(in the heart of lower town)

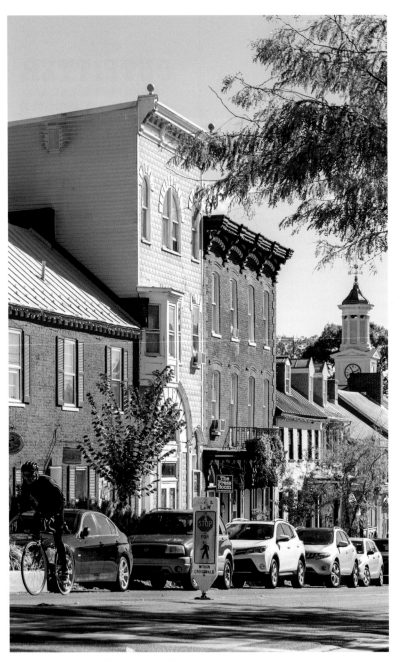

The Opera House on West German Street in historic Shepherdstown.

Photo: Jefferson County Convention & Visitors Bureau

SHEPHERDSTOWN

JEFFERSON COUNTY, WEST VIRGINIA

ELEVATION 300 FEET • C&O 72.8

The oldest town in West Virginia, Shepherdstown has 20 buildings that date from before the Revolution. The **Beeline March** from Morgan's Spring, located in today's Morgan Grove Park, to Massachusetts, 600 miles in 24 days, was the birth of the U.S. Army. After the horrors of Antietam came the **Battle of Shepherdstown** and the flood of 5,000 Confederate wounded who sheltered here for months. The **Rumsey Monument** commemorates James Rumsey's successful 1787 steam-powered vessel.

More than a dozen unique restaurants (no chains or national brands), from fine dining to casual, feature cuisine from many culinary traditions, most using local foods. Here, too, are more than thirty one-of-a-kind shops. Shepherdstown's hotel options include European luxury, Georgian elegance, and a historic inn. Live music, often free, is a Shepherdstown staple.

Shepherd University, home to 4,000 students, is central to town, and makes for a lovely side trip. Its art department has adorned the Duke Street Underpass with a life-size abstract painting that draws from local elements – like rolling mountains, rhododendron, wind turbines, and chimney swifts.

Fourteen preserved structures near Shepherdstown are on the National Register of Historic Places, including **Shepherd's Mill** (1739), **Boidstone's Place** (1766), and the **Van Swearingen-Shepherd House** (1773), and many are bikeable via local roads.

For details, check out **www.shepherdstown.info**.

Visit · Explore · Enjoy

TRAVELER SERVICES

WG	Welcome Center	304-876-2786
WG	Police Station / Town Hall	911
WG	Public Library 📶	
WG	Shep. Mystery Walks	301-639-0651
WG	Shep. Pedal & Paddle 🚲	304-876-3000
EG	Lucky's Barber Shop	304-870-4788
EG	NOVA Alternative Wellness	304-885-0093
EG	Roots Salon	304-870-3080
SP	Downstream to Wellness	540-336-4737
SP	Jefferson Security Bank 💲	304-876-9000
SP	Off Mane Street	304-876-6060
EW	Cool Green Auto & Tire	304-579-8920
EW	Post Office	
MX	Brown's Tire & Auto	304-876-6835
MX	Sheetz	304-876-2167
MX	Truist Bank 💲	304-876-3601
MX	United Bank 💲	304-876-6002
MX	Whale of a Wash Laundromat	304-294-9959

LODGING

A	Thomas Shepherd Inn 📶	304-876-3715
B	Bavarian Inn 📶	304-876-2551
WG	Mecklenburg Inn	304-876-2126

Also multiple guest houses - See Airbnb & Vrbo

GROCERY & SUPPLIES

WG	Farmer's Market (Sunday Mornings)	
EG	Grapes & Grains Gourmet	304-876-1316
SP	Community Garden Market	304-870-4230
SP	Qwik Chek Market	304-876-8484
EW	Shepherdstown Liquors	304-876-2100
MX	Dollar General	304-876-8230
MX	Food Lion	304-876-0601
MX	Rocs	
MX	Shepherdstown Pharmacy	304-876-9966
MX	Walgreens	304-876-0505

ART, JEWELRY & MUSEUMS

WG	Badgerhound Studio & Gallery	304-261-6028
WG	Civil War Center	304-876-5429
WG	Evolve	540-604-6703
EG	Cooper Captures	304-876-0910
EG	Historic Shep. Museum	304-263-3100
EG	KimoPics Gallery	304-582-1487
SP	Gallery at 105	304-876-8080
EW	Bridge Gallery	304-876-2300
MX	Christian Caine (Jewelry)	304-876-1313

DINING, DRINKS & ENTERTAINMENT

B	Bavarian Inn Restaurant 📶	304-876-2551
B	Bavarian Brothers Brewpub 📶	304-876-2551
WG	Bistro 112 (opening 2022)	
WG	China Kitchen	304-876-6620
WG	Kome Thai & Sushi Bistro	304-876-8798
WG	Rockhill Creamery	304-707-8765
WG	Shep. Opera House (opening 2022) 🎵	
WG	Shep. Sweet Shop	304-876-2432
EG	Betty's Restaurant $	304-876-6080
EG	Green Pineapple	304-870-4439
EG	Lilah Restaurant	304-470-4038
EG	Lost Dog Coffee	304-876-0871
EG	Maria's Taqueria	304-876-3333
EG	Mecklenburg Inn 🎵	304-876-2126
EG	Rainbow Connection Café 📶	304-870-2995
EG	Tommy's Pizza	304-876-2577
NP	Blue Moon Café 📶	304-876-1920
SP	Devonshire Café & Pub 📶 🎵	304-876-9277
EW	Alma Bea (opening 2022) 🎵	
MX	Dairy Queen	304-579-4999
MX	King's NY Pizza	304-876-0217
MX	McDonald's	304-876-1038
MX	Subway	304-876-1227
MX	A-wok	304-876-1088

SHOPPING

WG	Admiral Analog	304-491-6050
WG	Four Seasons Books	304-876-3486
WG	German Street Market	304-876-1106
WG	Honor D Fine Shoes & Hats	304-539-3236
WG	Meditative Medicinals	719-221-1543
WG	On the Wings of Dreams	304-876-0244
WG	Potomac Trading Co. WV	304-283-4109
WG	Reversa Rose Skincare	304-876-6555
WG	Threadz	
EG	Creative Procrastinations	410-917-7262
EG	Dickinson & Wait Craft Gallery	304-876-0657
EG	The Good Shop	304-876-8007
EG	Mountaineer Popcorn	410-937-4612
EG	Tonic Herb Shop	304-870-4527
SP	The Hive House	304-261-8548
EW	O'Hurley's General Store	304-876-6907

 WiFi  Live Music

 ATM  Bike Repair

Experience Shepherdstown

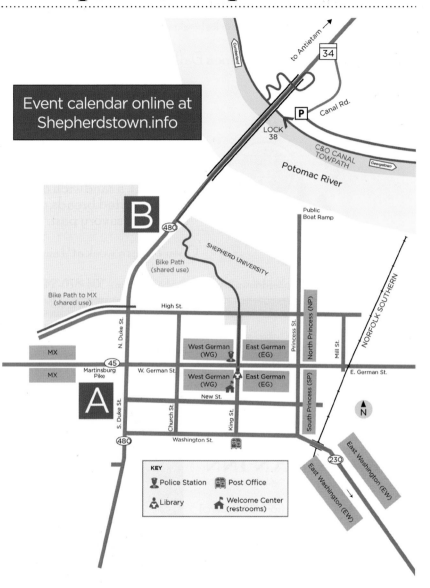

Event calendar online at Shepherdstown.info

to Antietam
34

Cumberland

P   Canal Rd.

LOCK 38

C&O CANAL TOWPATH   Georgetown

Potomac River

Public Boat Ramp

B   480

SHEPHERD UNIVERSITY

Bike Path (shared use)

Bike Path to MX (shared use)

High St.

N. Duke St.

Princess St.

North Princess (NP)

Mill St.

NORFOLK SOUTHERN

MX

West German (WG)   East German (EG)

45   Martinsburg Pike   W. German St.   West German (WG)   East German (EG)   E. German St.

MX

New St.

A   S. Duke St.   Church St.   King St.   South Princess (SP)

480   Washington St.

230   East Washington (EW)   East Washington (EW)

N

KEY

👮 Police Station   📮 Post Office

📚 Library   ⛪ Welcome Center (restrooms)

27 mi. Williamsport ◀•▶ Harpers Ferry 13.2 mi.

Thomas Shepherd Inn

Enjoy the gracious hospitality and delicious food of a classic bed and breakfast. Walk to dining, shops and entertainment.

300 West German St
Shepherdstown, WV 25443
www.thomasshepherdinn.com
304-876-3715 or 888-889-8952
info@thomasshepherdinn.com

THE INN AT ANTIETAM

SHARPSBURG, MARYLAND

The Inn at Antietam

A bed and breakfast with 5 suites with private bathrooms, surrounded by the Antietam Battlefield in historic Sharpsburg. Breakfast included, family friendly, dog friendly, WiFi.

2 miles from Lock 39, Snyders Landing – we can pick you up!
301-432-6601
www.innatantietam.com

Pedal & Paddle

Full service bike, kayak, and canoe shop providing sales, services, and rentals to locals and visitors since 2007. Experience riding a FAT Bike on the historic C&O Canal.

115 West German St
Shepherdstown WV 25443
304-876-3000
ThePedalPaddle.com
eddie@thepedalpaddle.com

Lilah Restaurant

Old favorites as well as seasonal and internationally inspired dishes and drinks. Wood-fired oven baked flatbread pizzas to seafood, pasta, char-broiled prime steaks, gluten-free and vegan options, and house made desserts. Dog friendly!

115 E German St
Shepherdstown, WV 25443
(304) 870-4038
lilah-restaurant.com

Williamsport's Cushwa Warehouse and Turning Basin allowed cargo to be loaded and unloaded easily from canal boats.

Photo: VisitHagerstown

WILLIAMSPORT

WASHINGTON COUNTY, MARYLAND

ELEVATION 380 FEET • C&O 99.4

The charming town of Williamsport sits on the banks on the **Conoco-cheague River** where it joins the **Potomac River.** Several B&B's, restaurants, taverns, pizzerias, and a delectable café welcome travelers. The C&O Canal National Historical Park's **Williamsport Vistor Center** is here, and the construction of the park's new headquarters is underway.

Cushwa's Warehouse, with its historic canal barge turning basin, serves as a gateway for cyclists to the town that was a busy inland port during the canal era. Coal was transferred from canal barges to rail cars after the **Western Maryland Railway** extended its line to Williamsport in the 1870's. The closure of the canal in 1924 served as an endpoint for significant development within the **Williamsport Historic District.** The result is a remarkably intact district of buildings from the initial settlement period to the heyday of the canal in the late 19th century.

The upstream wall of the three-arch **Conococheague Aqueduct** collapsed in 1920 as a boat was passing through it. The stone wall was replaced by a wooden one, serving the canal until it ceased operations permanently in 1924. A major improvement project, completed in 2019, reconstructed the 196-foot aqueduct to its pre-collapse appearance.

The eight-bay **Springfield Barn,** which overlooks Williamsport's **Byron Memorial Park,** was built in 1755 by Otho Holland Williams, the town's founder, and is one of the largest barns in the state. A museum located in its old milk parlor is open Sunday afternoons, March through October.

From **Doubleday Hill,** you can see all the canal features from one spot, including a lockhouse, a working lock, a Bollman bridge, and the **Turning Basin.**

For more information, visit **www.williamsportmd.gov.**

Located off East Potomac Street on Springfield Lane sits Williamsport's historic Springfield Barn and Museum.

Photo: Maggie Clingan.

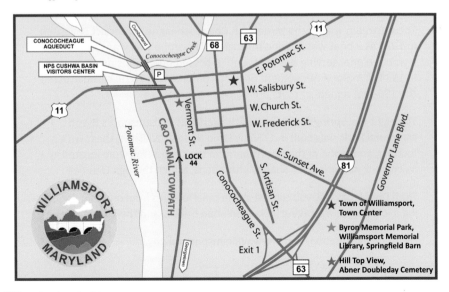

WILLIAMSPORT, MD: HONORING THE PAST, SHAPING THE FUTURE

CALENDAR OF EVENTS

For exact dates and up-to-date Calendar of Events go to
www.williamsportmd.gov | Facebook and Twitter @WilliamsportMD

Early May	**Williamsport Community Band's Spring/Celebration of Mothers Free Concert** – Springfield Farm Barn at 3pm
Late May	**Swimming Pool Opens** – 12noon-6pm – Enjoy!
Week of Late June	**Downsville Ruritans' Williamsport Carnival**— Bryan Park
Early July	**4th of July Celebration in the Park** – Byron Memorial Park Williamsport Community Band's Patriotic Concert at Dusk with a giant Fireworks display
Mid July	**Williamsport Bike Night** – Town Center – 5-10pm Concert, food, beer garden, vendors and more!
Late August	**46th Annual C&O Canal Days** – Arts, Crafts, Great Food, entertainment & much more! Located Town Center – Conococheague Street and Byron Memorial Park
Early October	**Harvest Hoedown** – 10am-4pm
Throughout October	**Williamsport's Haunted Walks October evenings** Full schedule will be on Facebook.com/Williamsportmd
Early December	**Christmas Parade & Byron Park Lighting 7-9pm.** Enjoy the Christmas lights of Bryon Park
Early and Mid December	**Christmas Events in Springfield Barn** – Bundle up – it's snowing in the barn – enjoy over 100 decorated trees, meet Santa & Mrs. Claus, check out "Buster the Talking Bear," train display, enjoy Reindeer Snacks, and take a horse drawn wagon ride around the Barn.
Early January	**Williamsport Polar Bear Plunge** – River Bottom Park Games start at 10am, Plunge at Noon Sharp!!

**Barn at Springfield Farm; Town Center is N. Conococheague St.
Byron Park is located off E. Potomac St., near Sheetz.**

Third Base Tavern

★ ★ ★ ★ ★ ★

Third Base Tavern

"Last stop before home."
"Such a great vibe – the kind of
bar where the employees/owners
make you feel welcome."

35 N Conococheague St
Williamsport, MD 21795
301-223-8274
Find us on Facebook Eds Third Base

Marco's NY Pizza & Restaurant

Home-style Italian food at great
prices. Specializes in New York Style
pizzas, pastas, subs, salads and
much more! Casual, family-friendly
dining room. Authentic Italian food.

20 Milestone Terrace • Williamsport
301-223-8820
marcosnypizza.com
Find us on Facebook

Still Smokin' BBQ

Provides eat-in, carry-out, delivery.
Catering service for your event
and can even show up in our food
truck. We look forward to seeing
you at our Williamsport location
or find us in our food truck.

24 N. Conococheague St.
Williamsport MD 21795
240-291-5406
stillsmokinbbq1@gmail.com
www.stillsmokinbbq.net

Desert Rose Café
& Sweet Shoppe

Located just blocks from the
C&O Canal. Serving soups, salads,
sandwiches, ice cream, sweets,
and full espresso bar. We also do
luggage and shuttles along the
entire length of the C&O Canal.

2 E Potomac St
Williamsport, MD 21795
desertrosecafeandcatering.com
301-223-6400

The C&O Canal Towpath approaching Hancock, at dawn.

Photo: Steve Dean

24.7 miles Williamsport
124.1 miles Washington D.C.

Cumberland 60.4 miles
Pittsburgh 209.2 miles

HANCOCK

WASHINGTON COUNTY, MARYLAND

ELEVATION 446 FEET • C&O 124.1

Centrally located and easily accessible to Interstates 70 and 68 and U.S. Routes 522 and 40, Hancock makes a great place to access the C&O Canal Towpath, the Tuscarora Trail, or the **Western Maryland Rail Trail** (WMRT).

Once the frontier edge of Maryland, Hancock has grown around transportation: from the **National Road**, the canal, the railroad, interstates, and now the trails. The canal reached Hancock by 1839 and Water Street, with all its wharves, was as busy as Main Street.

Today, travelers will find a full-service bike shop and shuttle service, restaurants, an inn, B&B's, two grocers, and other retailers.

In 1862 during the Civil War, Hancock resisted the siege led by famous General Thomas "Stonewall" Jackson in order to control major transportation routes in the area. For more on the area's history, be sure to visit the **Hancock Museum**, located in the town hall.

Limestone deposits were uncovered while building the canal and a cement mill was constructed about three miles west of Hancock. It later operated as **Round Top Cement Mill** and, by the 1860's, was Hancock's largest employer. The kilns and the foundations of the mill are still visible from the C&O Canal Towpath and the WMRT.

The WMRT parallels the C&O Canal for 26 miles. Many thru-trippers enjoy this asphalt-paved option, especially in inclement weather. The eastern end is near **Fort Frederick**, Maryland's first state park. The trail passes through Hancock at its mid-point and ends just past Little Orleans. See the map on page 98.

ATTRACTIONS 🅞
Trails, Rails & By-Ways
1 American Discovery Trail
1 Big Blue Trail
2 Civil War Heritage Trail
1 C&O Canal National Park Service Visitor's   301.678.5463
  Center (Bowles House)
1 C&O Canal Towpath Trail
1 Great Alleghany Passage (GAP) Trail
1 Great American Rail Trail
1 Great Eastern Trail
1 Potomac Heritage National Scenic Trail
3 The National Road
1 Tuscarora Trail
1 Western Maryland Rail Trail

Parks
4 Fort Tonoloway State Park   301.678.5622
11 Joseph Hancock, Jr. Primitive Camping Park   301.678.5622
80 Kirkwood Park (restrooms)   301.678.5622
13 Little Tonoloway Boat Ramp   301.678.5622
13 Little Tonoloway Recreation Area   301.678.5622
10 Major James Breathed Park   301.678.5622
6 Veterans Memorial Park   301.678.5622
12 Widmyer Park   301.678.5622

Museums
14 Hancock Historical Society Museum   301.678.5622
8 Hancock Tollhouse   301.678.5622
  (seasonal and special events only)
9 Hancock Veteran's Memorial   301.678.5622
14 Sideling Hill Exhibits   301.678.5622
16 Tonoloway Baptist Church   301.678.5622

VISITOR INFORMATION 🅞🅞
14 Hancock Municipal Office   301.678.5622
15 Hancock Post Office   301.678.6116

EMERGENCY SERVICES 🅞🅞
Fire-Rescue-Emergency   911
75 Potomac Chiropractic   240.343.8119
66 Home Center Pharmacy   301.678.5421
67 Reed's Pharmacy   301.678.2930
76 River Bend Family Medicine   301.678.7007
68 Maryland Vision Institute   301.791.0888
77 Tri-State Community Health   301.678.7256
78 Valley Health Hancock Family Medicine   301.678.6292
69 Veterinarian, Daniel A. Murphy   301.678.6635

LODGING & CAMPING 🅞🅞
28 Happy Hills Campground   301.678.7760
11 Joseph Hancock, Jr. Primitive Camping Park   301.678.5622
34 1828 Trail Inn B&B   301.678.7227
35 Hancock Motel   301.678.6108
38 Riverrun B&B   301.678.6150
40 Super 8 Motel   301.678.9717

BICYCLE RENTAL/SALES/SERVICE 🅞🅞
27 C&O Bicycle   301.678.6665

CAMPING & CAMPING SUPPLIES 🅞🅞
27 C&O Bicycle   301.678.6665
31 Mr. Hardware   301.678.5339
41 Dollar General Store   301.678.8110

42 Family Dollar Store   301.678.7352
24 Food Lion   301.678.6200
46 Sav-A-Lot Grocery Store   301.678.7612

RECREATION & TRAIL SERVICES 🅞🅞
27 C&O Bicycle (showers/restrooms)   301.678.6665
59 D&P Coin Operated Laundry   301.678.7141
62 Iron Tiger Fitness (call ahead for access)   240.446.9431
11 Joseph Hancock, Jr. Primitive Camping   301.678.5622
  Park (restrooms)
80 Kirkwood Park (restrooms)   301.678.5622
13 Little Tonoloway Recreation Area
  (restrooms/fishing)   301.678.5622
6 Veterans Memorial Park (restrooms)   301.678.5622
12 Widmyer Park (restrooms)   301.678.5622

FOOD & SPIRITS 🅞🅞
21 AC&T Convenience Store "The Market"   301.678.7327
45 Blue Goose Market & Bakery   301.678.5050
33 Buddy Lou's Eats, Drinks & Antiques*   301.678.6460
49 Hancock American Legion Post 26*   301.678.5961
50 Hardees   301.678.6307
82 Krazy Rayz Smokehouse   301.678.6208
51 Jimmy Joy's Log Cabin Inn*   301.678.5670
53 Park-N-Dine Restaurant   301.678.5242
86 Pittman's Liquor & Lottery*   301.678.5200
54 Pizza Hut   301.678.7217
44 Potomac Discount Liquors*   301.678.6787
48 Potomac River Grill   301.678.6100
25 Sheetz Convenience Store   301.678.6393
87 Subway   301.678.6193
56 Triangle Restaurant & Bar*   301.678.6175
57 Weaver's Restaurant & Bakery   301.678.6346
*sells beer, wine, liquor

BANKING & ATMS 🅞🅞
21 AC&T Convenience Store   301.678.7327
22 CNB Bank, Inc.   301.678.7205
23 M&T Bank   301.678.6132
24 Food Lion   301.678.6200
25 Sheetz Convenience Store   301.678.6393
26 BB&T Bank   301.678.5652

SERVICE STATIONS & AUTOMOTIVE 🅞🅞
21 AC&T Convenience Store and Gas Station   301.678.7327
73 Exxon Mobil Gas Station   301.678.6193
25 Sheetz Convenience Store and Gas Station   301.678.6393

SHOPS 🅞🅞
33 Buddy Lou's Eats, Drinks & Antiques*   301.678.6460
5 Hancock Antique Mall & Indoor Flea Market   301.678.5959
86 Loaves & Fishes Thrift Store   301.678.7553
87 North Bend Treasures Antiques & Gifts   301.678.2957
89 Rust N Found Antiques   240.291.1099

This project is sponsored by

www.townofhancock.org

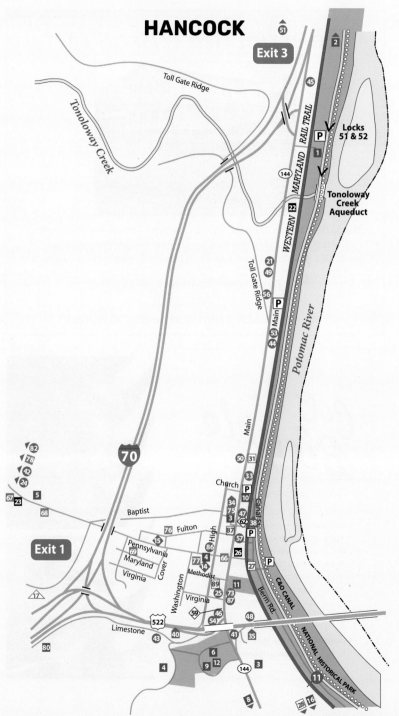

HANCOCK

Exit 3

Toll Gate Ridge

Tonoloway Creek

MARYLAND RAIL TRAIL

WESTERN

Locks 51 & 52

Tonoloway Creek Aqueduct

144

Toll Gate Ridge

Main

Potomac River

70

Church

Main

Baptist

Fulton

High

Pennsylvania

Maryland

Virginia

Cover

Methodist

Washington

Virginia

Canal

C&O CANAL

Berm Rd.

Exit 1

522

Limestone

NATIONAL HISTORICAL PARK

144

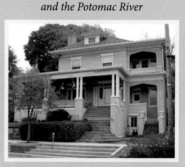
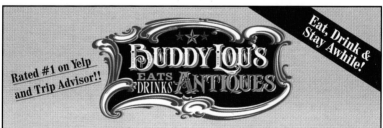

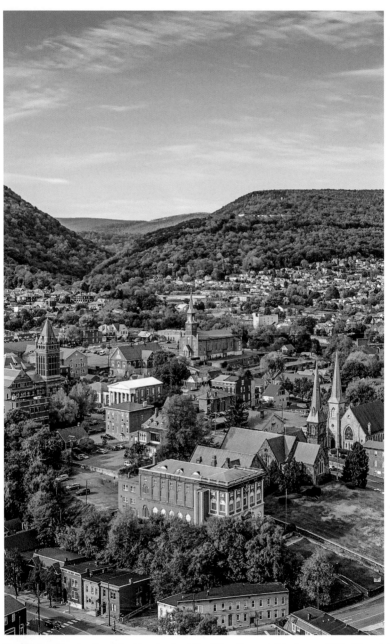

Downtown Cumberland, looking toward the "The Narrows" between Wills Mountain and Haystack Mountain.

Photo: Allegany Media

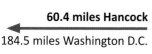

← 60.4 miles Hancock

184.5 miles Washington D.C.

Frostburg 15.5 miles →

Pittsburgh 148.8 miles

CUMBERLAND

ALLEGANY COUNTY, MARYLAND

ELEVATION 620 FEET • C&O 184.5 and GAP 0.0

Snug between the Potomac River and the rising Appalachian Plateau, Cumberland has long been a gateway for westward expansion. It marked the beginning of Delaware chief **Nemacolin's Path,** an ancient corridor through the rugged mountains, the eventual **Braddock Road**, a pre-Revolutionary path to move soldiers and goods to Fort Duquesne (now Pittsburgh), and its 19th century successor, the **National Road**. The railroads gathered at Cumberland, and today, both Amtrak and freight trains sound their horns before heading west.

The C&O Canal and Towpath terminate with a granite marker within **Canal Place Heritage Area**, home to the preserved **Western Maryland Railway Station** and the C&O Canal National Historic Park's Cumberland Visitor Center. Stop in for great exhibits, advice, and photos. Mile Zero of the **Great Allegheny Passage** is located under the arch.

From here, the GAP parallels the **Western Maryland Scenic Railroad**; both squeeze through the **Cumberland Narrows** formed by Wills Creek, and beneath **Lover's Leap**, a craggy overlook high above. Regular excursions on the WMSR take travelers and their bikes up to Frostburg via historic passenger cars, perfect for a day trip and ride back.

Today, a vibrant brick pedestrian mall along **Baltimore Street** boasts restaurants, art galleries, and gardens. Several hotels and B&B's make for excellent accommodations, and a nearby bike shop, outfitter, and several brew pubs add to the mix. The **Emmanuel Episcopal Church**, with its Tiffany stained-glass windows, sits on the site of the former **Fort Cumberland** and anchors the residential Washington Street Historic District. The **Allegany Museum** occupies the beautifully-renovated former post office and courthouse, and is open March through December.

For more information, visit **www.mdmountainside.com.**

VISITOR INFORMATION

Allegany County Chamber of Commerce	301-722-2820	D6
Allegany County Visitor Center	301-777-5132	G5
Cumberland Economic Development Corporation	301-722-4173	E7
City Hall/Main Street Office	301-759-6443	C6

RECREATION AND TRAIL SERVICES

Bike Lockers		H5
Cumberland Trail Connection	301-777-8724	H5
Cycles 'N Things	301-722-5496	B5
Fore Axes	240-362-7744	D8
Mountainside Bike Tours	301-722-4887	B9
WheelzUp Adventures	240-362-7021	E7

LODGING

9 Decatur Guest House & Hostel	301-722-4887	B9
Cumberland Inn & Spa	240-362-7111	G2
Fairfield Inn & Suites	301-722-0340	J6
Hampton Inn Cumberland	301-729-4028	G10
Inn on Decatur	301-722-4887	B9
Ramada Inn	301-724-8800	E9

FOOD AND DRINK

All That to Go!	240-362-7303	D5
Baltimore Street Grill	301-724-1711	E7
Basecamp Coffee Company	240-362-7022	G3
Café Mark	301-777-0037	E6
Caporale's Bakery	301-722-7755	E5
Charis Winery	240-581-3875	H5
Chopsticks	301-724-1082	D9
City Lights	301-722-9800	E6
Corner Tavern & Café	240-362-7534	B5
Crabby Pig	301-724-7472	H5
Culinaire Café of ACM	301-784-5413	D7
Curtis' Coney Island Famous Weiners	301-777-0380	D6
Dig Deep Brewing Co.	301-338-1013	H5
Domino's Pizza	301-722-0022	C8
El Jinete Mexican Restaurant	301-777-0847	A3
Ellie's Deli	301-724-5211	D9
European Desserts and More	301-777-0404	H5
Gianni's Pizza and Wings	301-722-0840	A4
Jin's Asian Cuisine	301-777-2233	C8
JJ's and Sons Pizzeria	301-777-3994	C5
Joe's Viaduct Restaurant	301-777-7500	A4
Klines Restaurant	301-777-5010	A3
Lost Mountain BBQ	240-362-7574	D7
M&M Bake Shop	301-722-2660	E7
McDonald's	301-722-4071	D8
Mezzos	301-777-7750	F8
Mise en Place	301-707-5086	D7
Niner's Canal Pub	301-777-1121	F6
Queen City Creamery	301-777-0011	F8
Ristorante Ottaviani	301-722-0052	D7
Roy Rogers	301-7777-8299	G9
Taco Bell	301-777-7021	H9
Uncle Jack's Pizzeria & Pub	301-724-1110	F6
Wendy's	301-759-3414	H8

ATTRACTIONS

Allegany Arts Council/Saville Gallery	301-777-2787	D7
Allegany Museum	301-777-7200	F6
Brooke Whiting House	301-777-778	E1
C&O Canal Visitor's Museum	301-722-8226	G5
Cumberland Historic Cemetery Association	301-722-4624	H1
Cumberland Railroad Museum	240-522-3670	H5
Cumberland Theatre	301-759-4990	D3
Embassy Theatre	301-722-4692	E6
Emmanuel Episcopal Church	301-777-3364	F4
Exit Strategy Escape Room	301-777-0747	F6
George Washington Cabin & National Road	Mile Marker 0	G4
Gilchrist Gallery	301-724-5800	E2
Gordon-Roberts History House	301-777-8678	E1
Loft 129	301-268-8619	E7
The Western Maryland Scenic Railroad	800-TRAIN-50	G8

EMERGENCY AND PUBLIC SERVICES

Amtrak Station	800-USA-RAIL	E9
City of Cumberland Police	301-777-1600	C5
City of Cumberland Fire Department	301-759-6485	C5
City Hall	301-722-2000	C6
Library, Allegany County	301-777-1200	E3
Post Office @ Pharmacare Pharmacy	301-724-1183	G3
U.S. Post Office	301-722-8190	F10

SHOPS

Allegany Liquor Store	301-777-7500	A4
Allegany Optical	301-722-6480	G4
Allegany Pawn	301-724-7296	E7
Auntie's Herb Shop	240-362-7663	E5
Awesome Gifts and Collectibles	301-777-7277	D7
Azad's Rug & Fine Arts Emporium	301-72300818	D7
Baltimore Street Collectibles	301-722-0344	E6
Barkin' Basement Thrift Shop	301-777-0826	E6
Bloom Box	301-722-4150	F6
Book Center	301-722-2284	D7
Buttercup Boutique	301-707-0369	A5
Cartridges Galore	240-362-7179	E7
Centre Street Collective	301-876-0667	D7
Craft Table	240-642-8828	E6
Cumberland Optical	301-722-4757	A5
Family Dollar	301-724-3408	C8
Fort Cumberland Emporium	301-722-4500	E6
Fruit Bowl	301-777-2790	A3
Graphicus Atelier	301-722-0018	E6
Hobbies Plus	301-777-1187	E8
Hometown Hobby Sports	240-362-7290	F6
Hush Skincare	301-724-0404	D7
Jacqie Q Photography	240-446-9928	E6
La Bella Vita	301-724-0404	E6
Lew Lew Belle Boutique	301-876-4466	E6
Maddcatt Vapors	240-362-7227	F9
Manhattan Golf & Gallery	301-777-0021	D7
Mid Centre Oddities & Antiques	301-338-4085	C6
Mixx112 Boutique	240-362-7273	F8
Morton's Jewelry	301-722-5710	E6
Next Level Mortal	240-920-8012	D6
Parkview Liquor Store	301-722-5257	F2
Roses Department Store	301-724-1345	C8
Sunshine Daze	301-697-5889	D6
Simplee Kountry	301-268-3052	H5
Terry's Jewelry	301-724-5115	E6
The Thrifty Baby	240-609-7538	E8
The Vapor Room	301-876-9500	D7
Western Maryland Music Center	301-724-1234	E8
Williams Stained Glass	301-722-0220	E7

OTHER SERVICES

Beckman's Greene Street Pharmacy	301-777-7336	F1
Community Acupuncture	240-920-9690	E7
Cuttz of Encouragement	301-338-1604	F6
CVS Pharmacy	301-724-5025	D8
KV Nails	301-722-1115	C8
Lifetime Eyecare	301-777-7777	D6
Martin's Market	301-777-7656	I9
PharmaCare West	301-724-1183	G3
Potomac Valley Pharmacy	301-722-2342	A5
Save-A-Lot Market	301-722-1100	
The Healing Tree Therapeutic Massage	301-784-6066	G8
Thrive Therapeutic Massage	240-920-0136	G8
Walsh, McCagh & Kellough Pharmacy	301-724-3646	C8

BANKING AND ATMS

BB&T (Truist)	301-777-4600	E7
Chessie Federal Credit Union	301-777-1781	E8
First People's Credit Union	301-784-3000	C8 & D8
First United Bank & Trust	301-724-8686	F8
M&T Bank	301-784-3101	D9
Standard Bank	301-722-5770	B4

CUMBERLAND

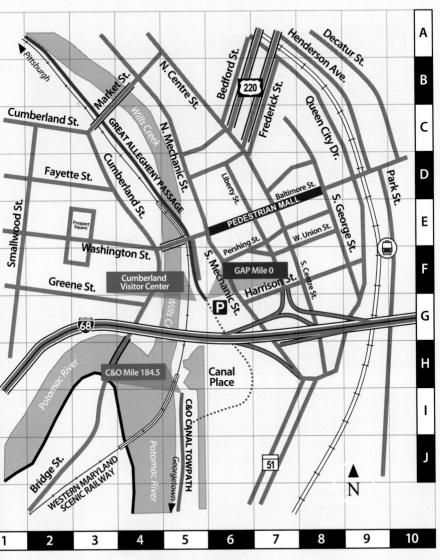

P Indicates Trailhead Parking

Cumberland
M A R Y L A N D

EXPLORE
the **ULTIMATE**
Trail Town!

Downtown Cumberland is the perfect base camp between Pittsburgh and Washington along the GAP Trail. Our mix of glorious turn-of-the-century streetscapes, unique local eateries/pubs and a flourshing arts community makes Cumberland perfect as an overnight off-ramp for long-distance treks or a destination hub for hiking or cycling day trips.

Check out or latest programming info online at www.MDmountainside.com or follow HistoricDowntownCumberland and VisitCumberlandMaryland on Facebook.

Just Getting Started or Final Destination?

Get a great night's sleep in one of our comfortable rooms or suites and enjoy thoughtful amenities, like on-site laundry, bike racks, and a bike wash station. Then, begin the next day with a wholesome, complimentary breakfast before you hit the trail again.

Complimentary Breakfast

Indoor Pool

Fitness Center

On-Site Laundry

Fairfield®
BY MARRIOTT

21 NORTH WINEOW STREET
CUMBERLAND, MD
301-722-0340 • marriott.com/cbefi

OWNED AND OPERATED BY   PLAMONDON HOSPITALITY PARTNERS

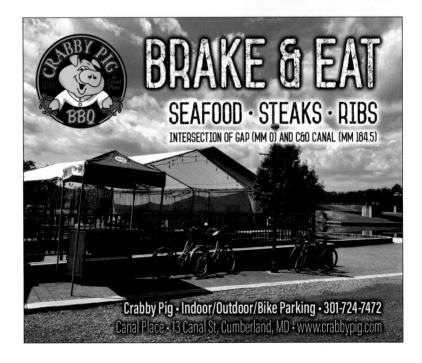

Wheelzup Shuttles and Adventures

Your one stop location for all things GAP and C&O.
We offer shuttles, rentals, repairs, gear and merchandise.

For reservations, call:
301-697-6577
or book online at
wheelzupadventures.com/shuttles-1

Ristorante Ottaviani

Serving steaks, chops, seafood, pasta and more. We offer a full bar, outdoor dining. Hospitality is our specialty, sempre famiglia. Open Tues–Sat, 5pm–close, large groups welcome, reservations recommended.

25 N Centre St, Cumberland, MD
301-722-0052
www.ottavianis.com

Hampton Inn Cumberland

Newly opened! Free hot breakfast in the morning, complimentary WiFi, sheltered bike parking inside, towels/water hose for cleaning. Relax from the GAP with us.

109 Welton Dr, Cumberland, MD
Only one mile from downtown
301-729-4028
Ask about the GAP rates!

Queen City Creamery & Deli

Try our famous, home-made frozen custard & sorbet along with sandwiches, soups and salads. Also breakfast & bakery items, lattés and specialty coffee drinks.

108 W. Harrison St., Cumberland
Full menu online at
queencitycreamery.com
Visit us on Facebook

Sunset car cruise along the National Road in downtown Frostburg.

Photo: Allegany Media

FROSTBURG

ALLEGANY COUNTY, MARYLAND

ELEVATION 1,832 FEET • GAP 15.5

With its cool temperatures and "college town" status, Frostburg is a mountainside oasis for GAP travelers. Originally a stagecoach stop along the **National Road**, it was once known for coal mining, and its employers still include a major manufacturer of ceramic fire bricks. Today, it boasts a vibrant year-round arts scene.

From the GAP, an amazing sculpture garden invites you up a switchback to the preserved 1891 **B&O Railroad Depot** – now the last stop for the **Western Maryland Scenic Railroad,** which transports passengers up from Cumberland. Across the street is the **Thrasher Carriage Museum**, which displays one of the top collections of horse-drawn vehicles in the country, representing every walk of life from the milkman to the wealthy, including pleasure vehicles, funeral wagons, and sleighs.

From the depot, walk your bike up the sidewalk to Frostburg's historic main street, and you'll find restaurants, coffee shops, ice cream stands and pizza joints, boutiques, galleries, a B&B, and a winery. You'll also see the 1897 **Gunter Hotel** and its 175-seat dining room, pressed tin ceiling, mahogany bar, and makeshift basement jail cell formerly used by federal agents when transporting prisoners during Prohibition.

Each April, the **Frostburg Arts Walk** showcases local artists, makers, and crafters via an outdoor walking tour. **Mountain City Traditional Arts** perpetuates Appalachian folk arts and presents a full calendar of performances, presentations, and workshops. Nearby **Frostburg State University**, home to some 4,700 college students, hosts the three-day **Appalachian Festival** every September; it features artisans, lectures, theater, food, and mountain music, and is worth a visit on its own.

Learn more about stopping here at **www.downtownfrostburg.com.**

CENTRAL BUSINESS DISTRICT

FOOD & DRINK

Clatter Cafe	240-816-7194
DeDi's Kitchen	689-3334
Domino's Pizza	689-8899
Eastern Express	689-5370
El Canelo	687-0750
Fat Boy's Pizza Shack	689-2727
Gianni's Pizza & Wings	687-1000
Giuseppe's Italian Restaurant	689-2220
LG's Pizzeria & Pub	687-0210
Lorenzo's Bakery	689-6570
Mountain City Coffee House & Creamery	687-0808
Outback Lounge	689-3831
Princess Restaurant	689-1680
Shogun Japanese Restaurant	240-284-2666
The Deep End	
The Main Street Pub	210-748-7052
TNT Dakota Saloon	268-1412
Toasted Goat Winery	240-558-9463
Route 40 Brewing & Distillery	
Gladstone Beanery & Creamery	

SHOPS & SERVICES

7-11 (with ATM)	689-6254
A Touch of Class	689-1030
Beer Wine & Spirits	689-1137
Cauldron Vintage	304-813-4367
Commercial Sound and Music	689-9505
The Country Diva Hair & Brow Boutique (2nd Floor of Hotel Gunter)	240-204-1102
Frostburg Fiber Depot	240-284-2154
The General Art Store	689-1234
Gladstone Mercantile	240-657-0500
Independent Ink Tattoo	689-1102
Jamaica Junction	689-6514
J. Bartles Jewelry	707-5133
J & S Gun & Pawn	689-6211
J.R.'s Custom Screen Printing and Embroidery	689-3604
Ladybug Boutique	
Lucky's Liquor Mart	689-6642
Madison Paige Boutique	240-580-7080
Main Street Books	689-5605
McFarland Candies	689-6670
Mountain City Traditional Arts	687-8040
The Nettle Patch	304-813-4912
Pet Wants	301-689-3909
P.S. Hair Design	689-1605
Sister's Choice	240-321-8607
Spectrum Designs, LLC	689-9748
The Vapor Room	689-6500
Wholesome Harvest Co-Op	689-3120
Window Expression	689-9009
Yellow K Record	240-284-2035
Z-Media	240-803-5920

LODGING

1	Allegheny Trail House	240-580-9795
2	Charlie's Motel	689-6557
3	Quality Inn & Suites	689-2050
4	Hotel Gunter	240-657-0500

5	Frostburg Inn	689-3831
6	Hampton Inn	689-1998
7	Trail Inn & Campground	689-6466

ADDITIONAL FOOD & DRINK

14	B&B Meat	689-6225
10	The Beach Club of Frostburg	240-623-6283
16	Burger King	689-5780
18	Frostburg Freeze	689-3020
19	Fox's Pizza Den	687-1003
21	Hurryback Inn	689-6557
22	Mario's Italian Eatery	687-1035
23	McDonalds	689-5099
25	Sand Springs Saloon & Steakhouse	689-8085
17	Snake Farm Barbacoa	904-762-8400
27	Subway	689-0011
28	Yamato Steak House of Japan	689-8888

ADDITIONAL SHOP & SERVICES

30	Dollar General	689-3712
26	EV Car Charging Stations	
29	EV Car Charging Stations	
31	Forever Nails	689-2299
32	Weis Market	689-6847
33	High Mountain Laundry	689-3333
34	Frostburg Health Center	689-3229
35	Frostburg Valero	689-1084
15	Get Out and Play Outfitters	876-7529
37	Harvey's Florist & Greenhouse	689-9266
39	Pharmacare of Frostburg	689-9961
40	Rite Aid	689-2422
41	Sav-A-Lot	689-9333
42	Sheetz Convenience Store (ATM)	689-3872
20	Steele Shears Studios	240-609-9548
45	Workman's Laundry	689-6800

ATTRACTIONS & RECREATION

43	21532 Mural	
36	Brownsville/Park Ave Memorial	
44	Community Model Railroad Club	689-6124
38	Evergreen Heritage Center	687-0664
50	Frostburg Dog Park	
8	Frostburg Museum	689-1195
	Braddock Stone	
9	Frostburg Pool	689-6000
56	Hoffman Hollow Park	
24	Mountain City Center for the Arts	240-357-0669
11	The Palace Theatre	687-0921
57	Parris N. Glendening Recreation Complex	
12	Sculpture Garden	
58	Sculpture Installation	
13	Thrasher Carriage Museum	724-4339
59	Tracks & Yaks	349-3699
15	Frostburg Depot and Turntable	

EMERGENCY & PUBLIC SERVICES

51	Frostburg Police	689-3000
	Frostburg Area Ambulance	689-3356
55	City of Frostburg	689-6000
52	Frostburg Public Library	687-0790
53	U S Post Office	689-6648

BANKING & ATMS

46	Al-Gar Federal Credit Union	689-6200
47	BB&T Bank - ATM	689-2277
48	First Peoples FCU	784-3000
49	M&T Bank	689-3182

All phone numbers are preceded by (301) unless otherwise noted.

FROSTBURG

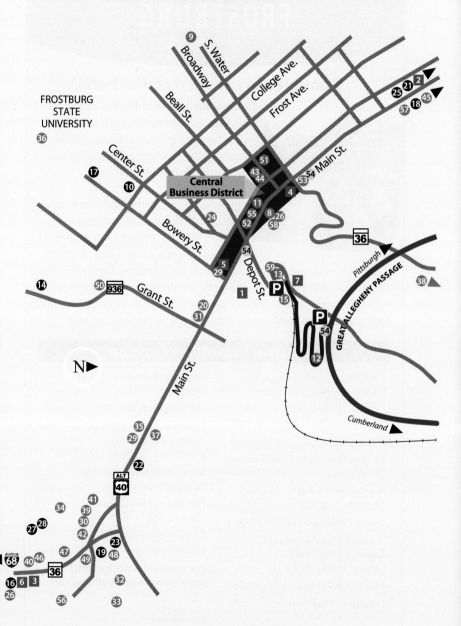

FROSTBURG STATE UNIVERSITY

Central Business District

GREAT ALLEGHENY PASSAGE

Pittsburgh

Cumberland

N►

P indicates Trailhead Parking

FROSTBURG

MARYLAND

Come see us...It's just cooler here!

The four-season community remains a welcoming and vibrant town to stop, shop, and stay. Home to Frostburg State University and nicknamed the "Mountain City," Frostburg boasts a bustling Main Street fittingly located up the hill from the Great Allegheny Passage.

Frostburg is a designated Maryland Arts and Entertainment District, which includes several galleries, Mountain City Traditional Arts, General Art Store, the historic Palace Theatre and the Frostburg Museum. The town has been listed on the National Register of Historic places, a Maryland Heritage Area, and named a "Maryland Main Street Community." You will find locally grown foods served in our finest restaurants, and you will have the opportunity to interact with the spirit of the town and the people that live here!

Join us in Downtown Frostburg

City Place Farmers Market
Fridays mid-May to October, 9:30am-1pm

Spring Arts Walk Saturday April 30

Pirates Ahoy! Wednesday July 6

Savage Mountain Punk Festival
Early August

Pig Out in the Park
Saturday August 20

Cruisin' Main Street Late August

Western Maryland Craft Beverage Festival
Sunday September 3

FSU Block Party Early September

Frostburg Dog Splash
September 10 & 11

FSU Appalachian Festival
September 18-20

Fall Arts Walk Early October

Winter Farmers Market
1st and 3rd Saturdays
November - April, 10 AM – 1 PM

Small Business Saturday
November 26

Frostburg Tree Lighting
November 27

Storybook Holiday
December 4

For more information, visit www.downtownfrostburg.com

Event dates are subject to change

The Western Maryland Scenic Railroad stops at the Frostburg Depot adjacent to the GAP.

Photo: Allegany Media

It's Just Cooler Here!

ONE HISTORIC LOCATION. FOUR REASONS TO VISIT.

Grab a morning coffee and muffin or enjoy a delicious lunch, dinner or Sunday brunch or stop in for a taste of locally crafted beer, wine or distilled alcohol in our Speakeasy tasting room. Shop in at Gladstone Mercantile and pick up a bottle or two of your favorite Toasted Goat or Route 40, as well as some pretty cool t-shirts, hats and outerwear. Hotel Gunter is also the perfect place for weddings, parties, reunions and more.

www.toastedgoatwinery.com • 11 W Main Street, Frostburg, MD • 240-558-9463

Commemorative mural by Diane Adams on the rear wall of Somerset Trust Company.

Photo: Great Allegheny Passage Conservancy

← **16.4 miles Frostburg**
216.4 miles Washington D.C.

Rockwood 11.9 miles →
Pittsburgh 116.9 miles

MEYERSDALE

SOMERSET COUNTY, PENNSYLVANIA

ELEVATION 2,106 FEET • GAP 31.9

Meyersdale sticks its reputation on being the center of the state's maple syrup production, with taps in backyards, farms, and woodlands for miles around. Its famous **Pennsylvania Maple Festival** runs for two weeks each March, and includes tours of Maple Manor (the historic Meyer Homestead), the crowning of the Maple Queen, a demonstration of syrup production at the Sugar Shack and Sugar Camp, an agricultural fair, a parade, and stacks of pancakes. No matter the season you arrive, make sure you leave room in your saddlebags for a few quarts of the good stuff.

For GAP travelers, Meyersdale is an ideal location. The **Keystone Viaduct** curves over **Flaughtery Creek** east of town, and the **Salisbury Viaduct** soars above the **Casselman River** to the west. The historic **Bollman Bridge** and the **Big Savage Tunnel** are a short ride away, as well.

In town, several magnificent B&B's, guesthouses, and a boutique inn await hikers and cyclists, and family restaurants, a drugstore, and a pizzeria serve up hearty meals. The **Maple Festival Campground** is open seasonally for those on a budget.

The **Meyersdale Area Historical Society** restored the 1910 **Western Maryland Railway Station** – "the finest station between Cumberland and Connellsville," according to the railroad's real estate agent, and this brick, semi-Tudor style building now houses a museum focused on the heritage of the area, specifically, the railroad, coal, and lumber industries. Friendly staff, a gorgeous model train setup, souvenirs, and snacks are available inside. A caboose newly painted in Western Maryland Railway colors is parked outside, next to bike parking and picnic tables.

Find out more at **www.visitmeyersdale.org**.

VISITOR INFORMATION

Meyersdale Area Merchants' Association   www.visitmeyersdale.org

27 Western Maryland Railway   814-634-8654
Station Visitor Center

LODGING & CAMPING

37	Donges Drive-In & Motel	814-634-5710
34	Levi Deal Mansion	814-289-7600
36	Morguen Toole Company	814-634-9900
15	Red Lantern B&B	814-442-6881
32	Trailside B&B	814-233-1991
40	Yoder's Guest House	814-634-8791
38	Maple Festival Campground	814-634-5710

FOOD & DRINK

4	Albright's Pizza & More	814-634-5120
37	Donges Drive-In & Motel	814-634-5710
52	Food Lion Grocery	814-634-0238
30	Fox's Pizza Den	814-634-7189
31	Fran's Bar	814-634-5269
24	G I Day Room	814-634-8624
36	Morguen Toole Company	814-634-9900
33	Pit Stop Kremery	814-634-9900
41	Sheetz Convenience Store	814-634-5138
7	Subway	814-634-1808
16	Take Six Pizza & Subs	814-634-9294
55	Tall Pines Distillery	814-442-2245
53	Traditions Catering	814-634-0839
47	White House Restaurant	814-634-8145

PARKS & ATTRACTIONS

5	Fuller Park, Playground & Pavilion, Farmers Market	814-634-8478
28	Maple Valley Park	814-634-5931
1	Mt Davis, Deer Valley YMCA and Highpoint Lake	814-662-4005
38	PA Maple Festival Park & Office	814-634-0213
2	Somerset Co. Fairgrounds	814-634-5619
60	Town Centre Park	

EMERGENCY & PUBLIC SERVICES

48	Meyersdale Ambulance Association	814-634-5956
12	Meyersdale Community Center	814-634-8478

45	Meyersdale Medical Center	814-634-5911
23	Meyersdale Public Library & Genealogy Center	814-634-0512
9	U S Post Office	

SHOPS & OTHER SERVICES

39	Apex Printing	814-634-5992
10	Clipped by Mandy	814-634-5385
54	Elk Lick Service Center	814-634-5159
65	Family Dollar	814-485-6044
6	Fine Wine & Good Spirits	814-634-8930
51	Gindy's Gym	814-634-0985
61	Hair Resque	814-634-5713
62	Lens Creek Studio	
26	Maple City Laundromat/ Tobacco Alley	814-634-0904
44	Maple City Muscles	814-634-9944
49	Maple Leaf Outfitters	814-701-8080
13	Meyersdale Automotive Center	814-634-5927
42	Meyersdale Country Bouquet Floral and Greenhouse	814-634-5979
43	Meyersdale Ministerium Association	814-634-5650
44	MRS Physical Therapy	814-634-5373
63	MS Shock Therapy	814-442-1191
18	New Republic Newspaper	814-634-8321
46	Quick'n Easy Autowash	814-624-3111
8	Roxie's Sheer Miracle	814-634-0970
3	Schafer's Candy	814-634-9720
35	Schafer's Floral and Gifts	814-634-0512
41	Sheetz Convenience Store	814-634-5138
21	Suder's Beverage Dist	814-634-8117
25	Thomas Drug Store (ATM)	814-634-8614
11	Treasure Hut	814-634-8516

BANKING AND ATMS

19	AmeriServe Financial Bank	814-634-5941
14	First National Bank (ATM)	814-634-8331
50	First Peoples Credit Union	814-634-9270
17	Somerset Trust Company (ATM)	814-634-1700

MEYERSDALE

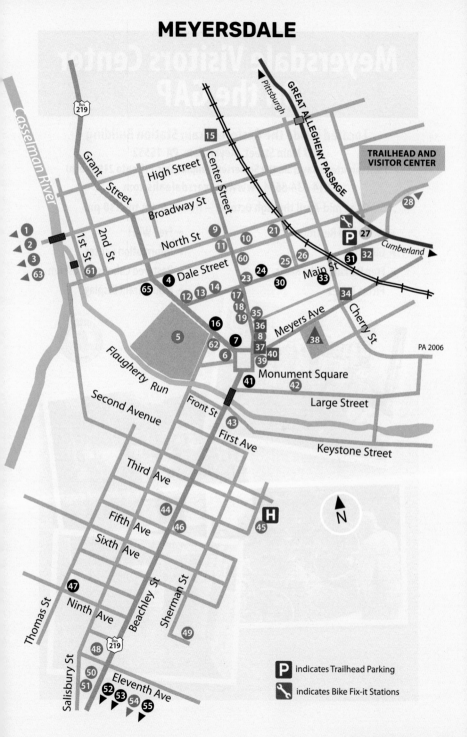

TRAILHEAD AND
VISITOR CENTER

Monument Square

P indicates Trailhead Parking

indicates Bike Fix-it Stations

Meyersdale Visitors Center On the GAP

Located Inside the Restored Train Station Building

527 Main Street, Meyersdale, PA 15552

(Just minutes away from the Somerset Turnpike Exit 110 onto 219 South)

814-634-8654 • www.meyersdaleahs.com

Open mid-April through October – Hours: 9 am to 4:30 pm

- ▶ Water and Restrooms
- ▶ Gift Shop
- ▶ Free Parking, Bike Racks, Picnic Tables
- ▶ Free Wi-Fi
- ▶ Information Center
- ▶ Restored Caboose, Museum
- ▶ Model Train Display

SPONSORED BY
SOMERSET COUNTY
TOURISM GRANT PROGRAM

GI Day Room Coffee Shop

GI Day Room

A local favorite since 1942! Located In heart of Meyersdale. Daily lunch specials, home of the smiley pancake, all-day breakfast, and amazing burgers!

309 Main Street, Meyersdale
814-634-8624
Mon. - Sat. 5:00 a.m. to 2:30 p.m.
Closed Sundays

Red Lantern B&B

Bike, hike, relax. Veteran owned. A gluten free B&B. Family friendly, great for small groups. We happily cater to special dietary needs. Ask about our military discount.

301 High St, Meyersdale, PA 15552
814-442-6881
redlanternbandb.com
redlanternbandb@outlook.com

SPONSORED BY

Garrett House B&B

Located at the top of the hill in Garrett PA, only 600 ft from the GAP. Historical architecture, owned and operated by seventh generation. Spacious and immaculately kept with guest access. 14 guests, 6 bedrooms.

508 Church St, Garrett, PA 15542
301-707-7182 • 240-321-5505
Book through airbnb.com

Overnight Camping

Maple Festival Park

A tent camping site is $20 per site, May – Oct, and offers space for one tent or hammock, restrooms with showers, WiFi, fire pits and firewood. Advance reservations: 814-634-0213 Email: pamaple@verizon.net. Same day reservations call: Susie Decker at 814-442-4284

120 Meyers Avenue
Meyersdale, PA 15552
Information at: pamaplefestival.com

Former mural along Water Street, Rockwood celebrating trail builder Maynard Sembower.

Photo: Paul g Wiegman

ROCKWOOD

SOMERSET COUNTY, PENNSYLVANIA

ELEVATION 1,826 FEET • GAP 43.8

At the foot of **Mt. Davis**, the highest point in Pennsylvania, Rockwood grew as the railroads expanded and was a lonely whistlestop along an isolated bend in the **Casselman River**. Today, whimsical, bicycle-themed metal sculptures greet you upon arrival, and GAP travelers will find B&B's, a hostel, a pizzeria, an antique shop, and a café, as well as a small-town shopping district. A walkable levy borders one side of its Main Street business district, and a residential neighborhood climbs the slopes on the other side. There's a well-kept private campground, too.

The **Rockwood Opera House** occupies a former grain mill, and from 1904 to 1921, showcased touring theater troupes, lecturers, and moving picture shows. Renovated in 2000 and reestablished as a beloved venue for live theater in a throwback setting, it's part of the **Rockwood Mill Shoppes** retail collective, and on the National Register of Historic Places.

On Market Street, the American Legion is spearheading the construction of the **Rockwood Veterans Memorial and Community Park** to honor the many soldiers, sailors, and airmen who valiantly served from the area. Four miles out of town each September – via a hilly on-road ride – is the **Farmers and Threshermen's Jubilee**, a country festival showcasing the early machines of agricultural life, from ponderous steam engines and early gasoline tractors to horse- and dog-powered machines.

Alternatively, you might consider pre-arranging transportation to the **Flight 93 National Memorial**, which honors the victims of the 2001 terrorist attacks on the United States and tells their stories. It's about 25 minutes away from Rockwood, the closest trail town, by car.

*Locations with WiFi access

ROCKWOOD

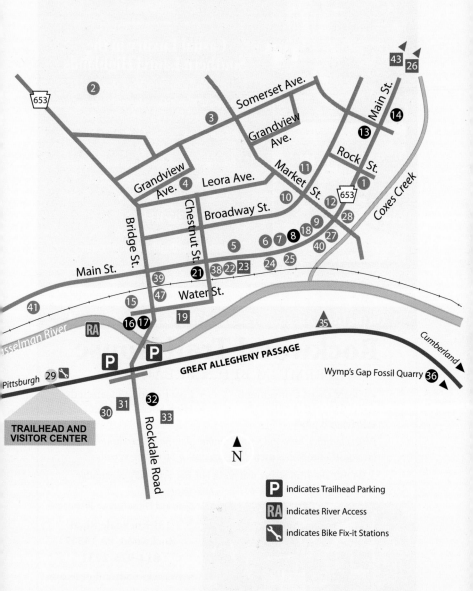

P indicates Trailhead Parking

RA indicates River Access

🔧 indicates Bike Fix-it Stations

Trailhead Brewing is a Craft Beer Brewery

Located at 402 Main St, Suite A, Rockwood Pa. The location is just .02 miles from the trailhead entrance. Trailhead Brewing has a taproom that offers delicious house beers as well as local wines and spirits. Call 814-926-2088 for hours of operation.

Also located at the same address is API Wash & Dry 814-926-2088

See, Tour, Capture

Somerset County's 42 amazing miles

- Three Trail Towns
- B&Bs and Hotels
- Flight 93 National Memorial

- Restaurants and Eateries
- Year-Round Attractions
- And Much More!

Let us help you plan your perfect ride

www.somersetpa.net

Gazebo in Confluence's Town Square.

Photo: Paul g Wiegman

CONFLUENCE

SOMERSET COUNTY, PENNSYLVANIA

ELEVATION 1,340 FEET • GAP 61.6

The **Casselman River** and **Laurel Hill Creek** join the **Youghiogheny River** in picturesque Confluence, a favorite stop for its many B&B's, guesthouses, restaurants, cafés, and an espresso shop, as well as access to great paddling, trout fishing, and wildflowers. Two bicycle/pedestrian bridges connect the town's peninsulas. A full-service bike shop and several retailers anchor its **Town Square**, itself reminiscent of New England with a lovely wooden gazebo perfect for a break from traveling.

Young George Washington explored the region in 1754 during his days as a surveyor, and noted that the three bodies of water together formed the shape of a turkey foot. To this day Confluence sits in the Turkeyfoot Valley, poised on the eastern edge of **Ohiopyle State Park** and its vast recreational opportunities.

Confluence is the home of the newly-opened **Joshua C. Whetzel, Jr. Recreation Area**, featuring an easy footpath up to a ridge overlooking the town and trail. The local can't-miss event is **Pumpkinfest**, an October weekend delight, with arts and crafts, live music, a pageant, an antique and classic auto show, square-dancing exhibition, and a largest pumpkin contest. The **Mt. Davis Challenge**, held most Julys, attracts road- and gravel-cyclists for a 56-mile race with punishing climbs to the state's high point and thrilling descents back to town.

A short ride from the GAP is **Youghiogheny River Lake and Dam**, with great views from the top of the dam and wooded picnic areas nearby. The popular **Outflow Campground** has a hiker-biker section and several loops for traditional car camping, and a nearby ice cream stop.

For a closer look, go to **www.visitconfluence.info**.

★   ★   ★

Find out more:

Confluence Tourism Association
814-395-9380 | www.visitconfluence.info

Visit us on Facebook
www.facebook.com/confluence.net/

Great Allegheny Passage
www.GAPtrail.org

*WiFi ◊ Beer/Wine/Liquor ☕ Ice Cream ⓘ Information rack

CONFLUENCE

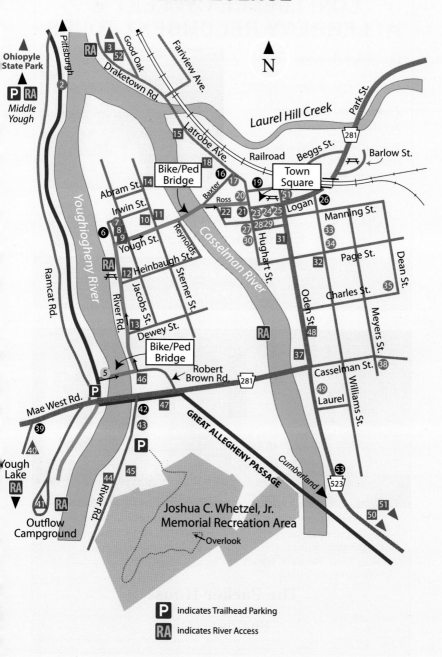

N

Ohiopyle State Park

P **RA** Middle Yough

Laurel Hill Creek

Town Square

Barlow St.

Bike/Ped Bridge

Bike/Ped Bridge

Youghiogheny River

Casselman River

Ramcat Rd.

River Rd.

Robert Brown Rd.

Mae West Rd.

GREAT ALLEGHENY PASSAGE

Yough Lake

Outflow Campground

River Rd.

Joshua C. Whetzel, Jr. Memorial Recreation Area

Overlook

Cumberland

Casselman St.

Laurel

P indicates Trailhead Parking

RA indicates River Access

Hanna House B&B

Rated #1 B&B in Confluence by TripAdviser. Full breakfast. Located 1/4 mile from Harnedsville Exit on the Bike Trail. Free shuttle to Confluence for dinner.

Frances Thompson
1790 Listonburg Road/Route 523
Confluence, PA 15424
814-395-9466
www.hannahousebandb.net

Cassleman Overlook

Cozy, cyclist-friendly guest house just 0.2 miles from the GAP trail. 3 guest rooms w/private baths, Kitchen, bike storage, decks overlooking the Casselman River.

Connie Spittal
726 Oden St, Confluence, PA
724-366-2503
conniespittal@hotmail.com
casselmanoverlook.com

Mitch's Fuel & Food

Full kitchen offering quick-casual service and seating with TV and Wifi featuring breakfast, fresh deli sandwiches, pizza, homemade soups and specials.

479 Latrobe Ave.
Confluence, PA 15424
814-395-3177
Open Daily 6 am - 9 pm
Visit us on Facebook

Confluence Cafe

World-class pizza, creative sandwiches, fresh salads. Vegan & gluten-free options. Dine in, on our patio, or borrow a picnic kit & enjoy the riverbank!

841 Oden St. Confluence PA
Order Ahead:
theConfluenceCafe.com
or call 814-704-0410

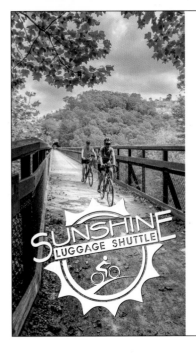

Loaded up near the Ohiopyle Low Bridge in Ohiopyle.

Photo: Great Allegheny Passage Conservancy

← **10.3 miles Confluence**
256.4 miles Washington D.C.

Connellsville 16.9 miles →
Pittsburgh 76.9 miles

OHIOPYLE

FAYETTE COUNTY, PENNSYLVANIA

ELEVATION 1230 FEET • GAP 71.9

Tiny Ohiopyle (pop. 59) has made its reputation as a whitewater paradise, smack-dab in the middle of famous rapids on the Youghiogheny River that once stymied George Washington's dream of a navigable route through the **Allegheny Plateau**. For decades, paddlers have come from all over the country to challenge themselves on this fast water.

Surrounding the town is beautiful **Ohiopyle State Park**, with 20,633 acres of hiking, mountain biking, rock-hopping, and vista-collecting. The first miles of the Great Allegheny Passage were completed within the park, and today, 26.7 miles of the GAP meander in its boundaries. The park's LEED-certified visitor center contains exhibits on local flora and fauna, the old train station features a themed escape room, and the **Ohiopyle High Bridge** carries the GAP over a hundred feet above the river. The GAP also crosses lovely **Ferncliff Peninsula**, a National Natural Landmark with short hikes and great views. The 70-mile **Laurel Highlands Hiking Trail** meets the GAP here, and **Cucumber Falls** (perhaps the most famous of the park's many water features) offers hikers a cool mist on a hot summer day. A new hiker-biker campground will be opened along the GAP in 2022.

Within Ohiopyle's densely-packed business and residential district are four family-owned outfitters which offer extensive excursion services for rafting, biking, or hiking, as well as a handful of restaurants, ice cream stops, guesthouses, and local shops. Pennsylvania's popular playground, **Seven Springs Mountain Resort,** is nearby. So is architect Frank Lloyd Wright's **Kentuck Knob,** a National Historic Landmark; his masterful **Fallingwater** recently received recognition as a **UNESCO World Heritage Site.** While both are close to the GAP, neither are bikeable. It's best to arrange a shuttle. Advance reservations are recommended, as well.

VISITOR INFORMATION

7 Ohiopyle Train Station Information/Restrooms

30 Ohiopyle Branch   800-275-8777
U. S. Post Office

36 Ohiopyle State Park Falls   724-329-8591
Area Visitor & Education Center

40 Ohiopyle State Park   724-329-8591
Ranger Station

LODGING & CAMPING

5 Falls Market, Restaurant   888-549-2017
& Inn

11 Ohiopyle Suites   724-329-8850

12 The Blue Heron House   888-549-2017

14 Stay In Ohiopyle   724-466-4613

15 MacKenzie Guest House   724-329-8531

16 Laurel Guest House   724-329-8531

17 Ferncli Guest House   724-329-8531

18 Hummingbird Guest Nest   724-329-5301
of Ohiopyle

22 The River House   877-574-7829

33 Heart of Ohiopyle   305-240-5909
Vacation House

34 Whitewater Adventurers   724-329-8850

42 Kentuck Knob Campground

RECREATION & TRAIL SERVICES

1 Fallingwater *   724-329-8501

2 Wilderness Voyagers,   800-272-4141
Rafting& Bike Tours

4 Middle Yough Takeout

6 Wilderness Voyageurs   800-2724141
Bike Shop

9 Kickstand Ice Cream   724-329-1450
& Bike Shop

21 Ohiopyle Zipline   724-329-8531
Adventure Park

29 Stewart On The Green
Community Playground

31 Laurel Highlands River   724-329-8531
Tours & Outdoor Center

32 Ohiopyle Trading Post   724-329-1450
& River Tours

34 Whitewater Adventurers   724-329-8850

35 Ferncli National Natural Area

37 Lower Yough Launch

39 Kentuck Knob*   724-329-1901

43 Ohiopyle Waterfall
Observation Decks

44 Laurel Highlands Hiking Trail (LHHT)

FOOD AND DRINK

3 Falls City Restaurant   724-329-3000
and Pub

5 Falls Market, Restaurant   888-549-2017
& Inn

8 Ohiopyle Candy Co., Frozen
Yogurt & Handmade Chocolates

9 Kickstand Ice Cream   724-329-1450
& Bike Shop

13 Ohiopyle House Cafe   724-329-1122
& Tavern

24 Beef Jerky Experience   412.996.8729

26 Ohiopyle Bakery &   724-329-2253
Sandwich Shoppe

26 Bite My Weiner Famous   724-329-2253
Ohiopyle Dog Shack

27 Paddler's Pizza   724-329-8888

41 Bittersweet Café   724-329-4411

EMERGENCY SERVICES

19 Ohiopyle-Stewart V.F.D.   724-329-4891

SHOPS AND OTHER SERVICES

10 Ohiopyle Suites Laundromat 724-329-8850

20 T'nkr

23 Oddly Enough   724-557-2125

25 Ohiopyle-Stewart
Community Center

28 24-Hour ATM (Somerset Trust)

38 Ohiopyle Adventure   412-558-0274
Photography

*Not accessible by bicycle, call for shuttling options

OHIOPYLE

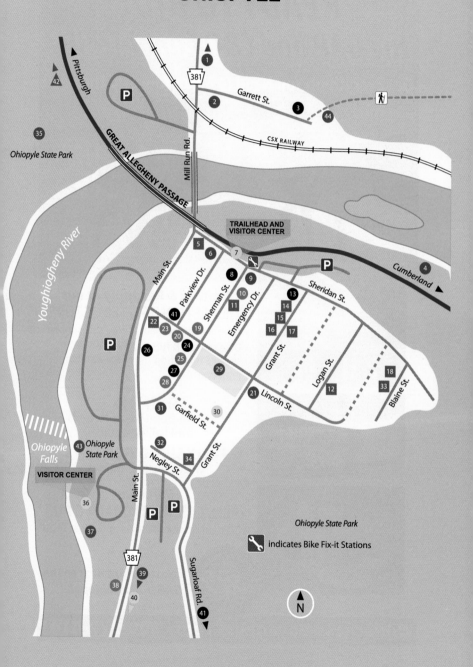

Pittsburgh

42

381

1

Garrett St.

2

3

44

CSX RAILWAY

35

Ohiopyle State Park

Mill Run Rd.

GREAT ALLEGHENY PASSAGE

Youghiogheny River

TRAILHEAD AND
VISITOR CENTER

5

6

7

Cumberland

4

Main St.

Parkview Dr.

8

9

Sherman St.

10

11

Emergency Dr.

Sheridan St.

13

14

15

16

17

Grant St.

Logan St.

41

22

23

20

19

24

25

18

33

Blaine St.

26

27

28

29

12

31

30

Garfield St.

21

Lincoln St.

Ohiopyle
Falls

43

Ohiopyle
State Park

32

34

Negley St.

Grant St.

VISITOR CENTER

Main St.

36

37

381

38

39

40

Sugarloaf Rd.

41

Ohiopyle State Park

indicates Bike Fix-it Stations

N

Ohiopyle Bakery & Sandwich Shoppe

A must stop for homemade baked goods – baked fresh daily, deliciously healthy deli fresh sandwiches – made to order. Salad or melt-in-your-mouth cookies! We can't wait to see you, come visit us soon!

85 Main St, Ohiopyle, PA 15470
724-329-2253
ohiopylebakery.com

Ohiopyle Suites

Newly updated and remodeled, the Ohiopyle Suites offers accommodations that are in the heart of Ohiopyle. Bicycle friendly, great for groups and bike tours. There are 10 one bedroom units and five two bedroom units.

22 Sherman St, Ohiopyle PA 15470
724-329-8850
www.wwaraft.com

Beef Jerky Experience

Do you love jerky? We offer more flavors of jerky than you have ever dreamed of! In addition to our mouth-watering jerky, we have snack sticks, dried fruits, local, canned and pickled items, jerky making kits, seasonings, hot sauces, jerky chew, and more!

Ohiopyle-Stewart Community Center
15 Sherman St., Ohiopyle, PA 15470
(412) 996-8729

PRESENTED BY:
UPMC HEALTH PLAN

P3R

The GAP Relay presented by UPMC Health Plan is an unforgettable adventure relay race between Pittsburgh, PA and Cumberland, MD! Build your team and set out to conquer a 150-mile journey that will challenge you in ways you didn't know were possible!

810 River Ave, Pittsburgh PA 15212
412-586-7785
info@p3r.org gaptrailrelay.org

A statue of surveyor and Revolutionary War hero Col. William Crawford stands outside the historic Carnegie Free Library in Connellsville, Pa.

Photo: Allegheny Trail Alliance

CONNELLSVILLE

FAYETTE COUNTY, PENNSYLVANIA

ELEVATION 915 FEET • GAP 88.8

The charming city of Connellsville sits just past the western edge of **Ohiopyle State Park**, and welcomes travelers seeking rest and replenishment. With a trailside hotel and several magnificent B&B's, plus restaurants, a bike shop, and ice cream stops, it's a favorite GAP stop.

During the **French and Indian War**, British General Edward Braddock bivouacked at Connellsville (then known as Stewart's Crossing) with his men – including young aide-de-camp George Washington – before their fateful march toward Ft. Duquesne. Local history buffs reenact this river crossing each June.

In the 19th and 20th centuries, because of the presence of the **Connellsville Coalfield** – part of the most extensive, purest metallurgical sources of coal in the United States – coal mining and coke manufacturing fueled Connellsville's economy, and the city once boasted more millionaires than any city its size. A score of Victorian mansions and soaring churches recall that era.

The GAP follows Third Street through the west side of town via separated bike lanes, passing by the grotto at **St. Rita's Catholic Church**, built from Youghiogheny River stone by parishioners beginning in 1932. A side trip using Crawford Street yields a great tour of public murals and the **Connellsville Canteen**, which showcases the lives of local veterans and features a model train exhibit. Follow the **Connellsville Bike Loop** for a neighborhood tour (green signs) or the business district (purple signs).

On the way out of town, you'll pass under a colorful 14-foot arch designed and built by artist Steven Fiscus which features stained glass made in the town's own **Youghiogheny Opalescent Glass Factory**, perfect for a picture.

VISITOR INFORMATION

69	Connellsville Chamber of Commerce	628-5500
2	Connellsville Caboose Welcome Center	
71	Connellsville Canteen	603-2093
27	Connellsville Visitors Center	

LODGING

3	Adirondack Shelters	
11	Comfort Inn	603-3580
19	Connellsville B&B	603-2533
1	Uniontown KOA at River's Edge (Mile 92)	628-4880
30	River House Airbnb	
23	Seams Like Home Retreat	984-1399

RECREATION & TRAIL SERVICES

29	Bikes Unlimited	628-2453
81	Sheepskin Trail (at GAP Mile 87)	
25	Spotto's Sporting Gear	628-7060

FOOD AND DRINK

44	The Arch Café	628-9117
10	Bloom Brew	317-1895
10	Bloom Brew Draft Wagon	
49	Bud Murphy's Sports Bar	628-9884
63	Clubhouse Pizzeria	603-2637
8	Colebrook Chocolates	628-8383
32	Cole B's	603-2992
51	Domino's Pizza	620-0123
59	Double Dragon Chinese Restaurant	628-7449
68	Fox's Pizza Den	620-2803
46	Dunkin'	603-2700
39	Great Wall Chinese Restaurant	628-9730
42	Hometown Diner	628-7006
47	The Italian Oven	626-6836
16	Keedy's Pizzeria	603-2929
37	Kickstand Kitchen	603-3777
43	Little Caesars Pizza	626-1530
48	McDonald's	626-1442
9	NY Pizza and Pasta	628-4946
31	New Haven Trailside Treats The Outpost River's Edge Eatery	628-4792
56	The Paint Room Restaurant	626-9532
55	Pechin's Deli	628-7400
18	Ruvo's	320-5059
13	Sheetz Convenience Store (ATM) 24/7	628-8044
12	Valley Dairy Restaurant	626-8798
24	Wendy's	628-3373

GROCERY, PHARMACY, LAUNDROMAT

40	Cash Saver	628-9893
10	Curtis Pharmacy	626-1091
4	Martin's Supermarket and Deli 6 am – Midnight	628-802
41	Nickman Drug	628-812
55	Pechin's Deli	628-740
45	Rite Aid	628-846
33	West Gate Cleaning Village (Laundromat)	628-689

PARKS & ATTRACTIONS

5	Colonel Crawford's Cabin	
79	East Park	
62	Lions Square Park	
71	Model Railroad Display & Canteen	
6	Yough River Park (Wi-fi)	

EMERGENCY & PUBLIC SERVICES

53	Amtrak Station	800-USA-RA
78	Carnegie Library – Internet Access	628-138
66	Community Ministries	626-112
60	Connellsville City Hall	628-202
67	Fayette EMS	91
52	Highlands Hospital	628-150
60	Police Department	91
57	U.S. Post Office	628-729

SHOPS & OTHER SERVICES

28	All Doll'd Up	
70	Appalachian Creativity Center	208-174
34	The Book Case	628-918
36	Coldwell Banker Laurel Ridge Realty	628-720
70	Coterie	562-068
20	Connellsville Massage	710-934
7	Dollar Tree	626-162
15	Mug N Brush Fitness Center & Gift Shop	628-395
72	Pat's Bridal Boutique	628-617
21	Riverwalk Antiques	707-955
26	Spotto's Hardware	628-801
74	T&A House of Treasures	875-192
50	Phoenix Salon	603-218
58	Wavie and Jane's	626-126
17	Youghiogheny Holistic Living	707-433

BANKING & ATM

76	cfsbank	628-600
54	Glass Cap Federal Credit Union	628-242
22	PNC Bank – ATM	888-762-226
38	PNC Bank – Shopping Plaza ATM	628-125
75	Scottdale Bank and Trust, a Mid Penn Co	628-320
14	Somerset Trust	620-413

All phone numbers are preceded by (724) unless otherwise noted.

CONNELLSVILLE

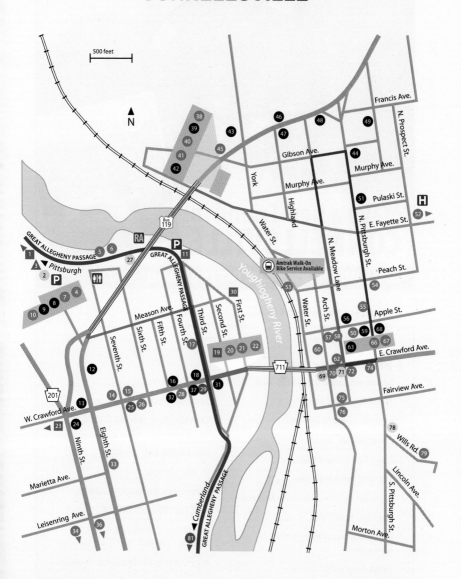

500 feet

N

Francis Ave.

N. Prospect St.

Gibson Ave.

York

Murphy Ave.

Murphy Ave.

Highland

Pulaski St.

N. Pittsburgh St.

E. Fayette St.

H

Water St.

GREAT ALLEGHENY PASSAGE

Pittsburgh

P

Bus 119

RA

P

GREAT ALLEGHENY PASSAGE

Amtrak Walk-On Bike Service Available

Peach St.

Youghiogheny River

Water St.

Arch St.

N. Meadow Lane

Meason Ave.

Fifth St.

Fourth St.

Third St.

Second St.

First St.

Apple St.

E. Crawford Ave.

Sixth St.

Seventh St.

711

201

W. Crawford Ave.

Fairview Ave.

Eighth St.

Ninth St.

Wills Rd.

Marietta Ave.

Lincoln Ave.

S. Pittsburgh St.

Leisenring Ave.

Cumberland

GREAT ALLEGHENY PASSAGE

Morton Ave.

CONNELLSVILLE BIKE LOOP – The loop involves riding with traffic. Wear a helmet and exercise caution.

ROUTE DETAILS At the intersection of W. Fayette Street and N. Meadow Lane, the bike loop splits. To the right is the neighborhood path (in GREEN), and to the left is the local business loop (in PURPLE) to get to Downtown Connellsville. A route to and from Connellsville's Amtrak station (in ORANGE) connects to the main bike loop at N. Meadow Lane.

P indicates Trailhead Parking   **RA** indicates River Access

Make a New Friend in
CONNELLSVILLE

ONLY 60 MILES FROM PITTSBURGH

▶ **CONNELLSVILLE HAS IT ALL**

History and Museums   Bike and Gift Shops   Hospital
Restaurants and Lodging   Art and Antiques   Concerts and Events

▶ **2022 LOCAL EVENTS**

Downtown Connellsville Soup Walk – March 5

Yough River Trail Race – April 16

Connellsville Yard Sale– May 7

Amish Donuts– May 7

Lion's Club Rabies Clinic – May 7

Fayette County Train Day – May 14

Connellsville Geranium Festival – May 28

City Food Truck Event – May (tentative)

Recreation Board Wine Festival –
May (tentative)

Yough River Rally – June 3, 4, 5

Lion's Kids Festival – June 6

Lion's Club Concert Series –
Sundays June/July/August 7pm-9 pm

Braddock's Crossing – June 25, 26

Somerset Trust Car Show – June 28

Connellsville Rockin' Rib Festival –
July 2, 3, 4 (tentative)

Woodruff 5k Run – July 14

St. Rita's Festival – July 7, 8, 9

Wellness on the Yough – September 3

YRTC Fall Foliage Ride/Walk – October 3

**Downtown Connellsville Chili
Festival** – November 5

It's a Connellsville Christmas – December 3

www.connellsville.us

www.downtownconnellsville.org

Kickstand Kitchen

Offering fun sandwiches, large fresh salads, homemade soups, shareable plates. BYOB, free wifi, bicycle parking, outdoor seating, eat in or take out.

507 W Crawford Ave 724.603.3777
Located right off the Great Allegheny Passage in Connellsville
kickstandkitchen.com

Connellsville Bed & Breakfast

Each room has a private bath and the breakfasts are filling and delicious. A locked garage with bike stand, tools, hose and towels. Coin-operated laundry available. 150 feet from the trail and only 375 feet from restaurants.

316 W. Crawford Avenue
Connellsville, PA 15425
724-603-2533
connellsvillebedbreakfast.com

Bikes Unlimited

Bike rentals right along the GAP trail! Family owned since 1987. Mechanical work. Mt Bikes, Recumbents, Trikes, plus accessories & clothing. Open Tuesday - Sunday.

503 W. Crawford Ave
Connellsville, PA 15425
724-628-2453
www.bikesunlimited.biz

Colebrook Chocolate

Delight the senses with chocolates & confections from Colebrook Chocolate Co. Summertime treats include ice cream cones and old-fashioned malts & milk shakes.

724-628-8383
830 Vanderbilt Road
Connellsville, PA
(In the Martin's Shopping Plaza)
Just steps off of the GAP Trail

The reconstructed Pittsburgh & Lake Erie train station now serves as a visitor center along the Great Allegheny Passage in West Newton.

Photo: Great Allegheny Passage Conservancy

WEST NEWTON

WESTMORELAND COUNTY, PENNSYLVANIA

ELEVATION 769 FEET • GAP 114.1

With four bed-and-breakfasts, several restaurants, a full-service bike shop, canoe livery, craft brewery, bakery, and new distillery, West Newton is the quintessential trail town along the Great Allegheny Passage, and a favorite stop for thru-riders.

The **Youghiogheny River** calms here, and in 1788, New England pioneers, led by Revolutionary War veteran Gen. Rufus Putnam, launched flatboats to begin a final exploratory push to settle in the Ohio Territory. The town's early name, "Simeral's Ferry," lives on in today's **Simeral Square**, a delightful picnic and gathering space overlooking the river.

West Newton's first and biggest industry was the **Markle Paper Mill**, opened in 1859 to supply the region with quality paper. Wood pulp came from a mill in Markleton, Somerset County. After the mill closed in 1893, the building was purchased by the U.S. Radiator Company, which made heating radiators here until 1955. The building still stands on North Water Street. The 1814 clapboard **Plumer House**, on South Water Street and the oldest structure remaining in West Newton, is on the National Register of Historic Places. So is the **Banking House of Mungo Dick**, a Queen Anne style brownstone on Main Street, built in 1890. The 45-acre **West Newton Cemetery** makes for a great walking tour, and is regarded as one of the most beautiful cemeteries in Pennsylvania by numerous veterans' groups.

Along the GAP, the **West Newton Visitor Center** occupies a recently-built reconstruction of the Baltimore and Ohio train station that once served rail passengers. Its friendly staff, clean bathrooms, and array of GAP merchandise make it an attractive stop. Sign the guestbook, place a pin indicating your hometown in the wall map, and take a photo in front of the preserved Pittsburgh and Lake Erie passenger car parked outside.

VISITOR INFORMATION

| 40 | Downtown West Newton, Inc | 872-0100 |
| 1 | West Newton Visitor Center* | 872-5586 |

LODGING & CAMPING

7	Bright Morning B&B	872-0792
58	Cedar Creek Campground (3 miles south on trail)	872-5586
2	GAP Trail Campground	244-5859
7	The Annex Inn	872-0792
7	Willow Springs Lodge	872-0792

RECREATION & TRAIL SERVICES

| 24 | West Newton Bicycle Shop | 872-2185 |

FOOD AND DRINK

10	Bloom Brew Brewery	322-4494
10	Bloom Brew Draft Wagon	
45	Crooked Creek Distillery and Smokestack BBQ	244-1866
26	Fox's Pizza Den*	872-4442
43	Gary's Chuckwagon Restaurant*	872-8920
43	Gingerbread Bakery & Le Grande Catering	872-8920
13	Letterio's Beer and Beverage	872-9466
22	Mama Pepino's Pizza	872-0338
11	The Outpost River's Edge Eatery	
31	Subway Restaurant	633-0084
23	The Trailside* – Restaurant, Pub	872-5171
44	West Newton Pizza House	872-6909

GROCERY, PHARMACY, & LAUNDROMAT

4	Giant Eagle	872-5443
8	Rite Aid Pharmacy	872-6401
12	Riverside Laundry (24/7)	

PARKS & ATTRACTIONS

56	Community Swimming Pool	872-9222
5	Goehring Park & Ballfields	
25	Historic West Newton Cemetery	872-7883
19	Lions' Field	
27	Simeral Square Park	
50	Vine Street Park	

EMERGENCY & PUBLIC SERVICES

37	Borough Offices	872-68(
37	Police	9
14	WN Public Library*	633-079
47	U.S. Post Office	872-61(
10	Volunteer Fire Company	872-60(
44	West Newton-Rostraver Ambulance	872-31
28	Center for Active Adults*	872-49

SHOPS

34	Back in the Attic Consignment Shop	
61	Joe's Tackle Unlimited	412-735-97(
39	Mantle House Mission	872-71
36	Miss Claire's Treasure Gift Shop	
60	Touched By Time Antiques	
54	Tull's Florist	872-67(
41	Tumbledown Collectibles	633-00-
51	William's Ace Hardware	872-778

OTHER SERVICES

33	Art Vac Signs	872-77;
46	Barb's Dog Grooming	872-70!
47	Contemporary Design	872-10(
17	George's Tire Service	872-44-
16	Maria's Alterations & Dry Cleaning	872-45
6	Martinelli's Auto Service	872-40;
42	Meghan Pogyor's Barbershop	
9	Speney Sales & Service	872-77(
52	Sunoco Service Station	872-11(
53	West Newton Animal Clinic	872-86-
3	West Newton Piano & Voice	872-83(
30	Village Print Shop	872-41(

BANKING & ATMS

| 29 | Commercial National Bank (ATM) | 872-51(|
| 38 | PNC Bank (ATM) | 872-40- |

*Locations with WiFi access

All phone numbers are preceded by (724) unless otherwise noted

WEST NEWTON

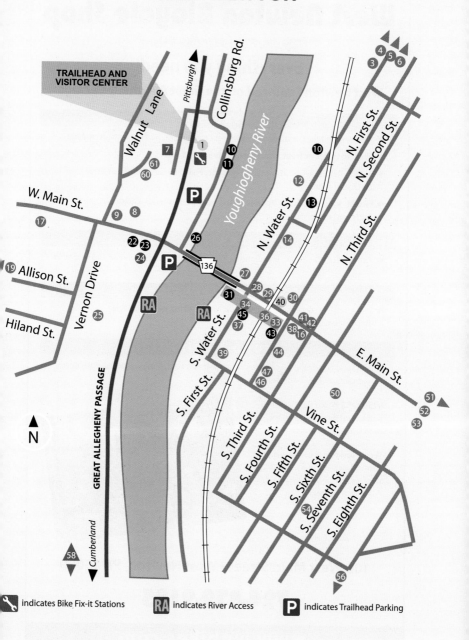

TRAILHEAD AND VISITOR CENTER

Walnut Lane

Pittsburgh

Collinsburg Rd.

Youghiogheny River

W. Main St.

N. First St.

N. Second St.

N. Third St.

N. Water St.

Allison St.

Vernon Drive

Hiland St.

136

S. Water St.

S. First St.

GREAT ALLEGHENY PASSAGE

E. Main St.

S. Third St.

S. Fourth St.

S. Fifth St.

Vine St.

S. Sixth St.

S. Seventh St.

S. Eighth St.

N

Cumberland

indicates Bike Fix-it Stations   RA indicates River Access   P indicates Trailhead Parking

West Newton Bicycle Shop

"By Bike Riders for Bike Riders"

Everything *you* need!

West Newton Trailhead on the Great Allegheny Passage

SALES

- ◆ New & used bikes, trailers, apparel,safety equipment, parts, gear & accessories
- ◆ **We can meet or beat almost any advertised price!**
- ◆ **BIKES:** Recumbents, Mountain, Freestyle, Hybrids, Comfort, Cruisers, BMX and more
- ◆ **FROM**: Raleigh, Marin, Redline, Haro, Sun, EZ Racers, Bachetta, Surly and more

SERVICE

- ◆ Full service bike shop , installations, repairs, changes, adjustments and assembly

RENTALS

- ◆ Bikes, trailers, & combos - hourly, daily, and group rates available Recumbents, Trikes, Tandems

FOOD & DRINKS

- ◆ Hot food & drinks, snacks, ice cream, pop and cold drinks, vending and more (upstairs at The Trailside)

VISITORS - Two B&B's within blocks and over 25 hotels and motels within 12 miles

West Newton store open year round Located on Rt. 136 @ the intersection of bridge and Great Allegheny Passage

106 West Main Street • West Newton, PA 15089

724-872-2185

www.wnbikes.com

Adele's Bed & Breakfast

Just 0.2 miles from the GAP trail and offers quaint accommodations. Five rooms are available with a three bedroom apartment for larger groups. Secure parking for bicycles.

138 First Street, Smithton, PA 15479
724-872-6279
Find us on Facebook
and tripadvisor

Bright Morning B&B

Lodging, eating and drinking on the GAP since 2001. Four late Victorian/Federalist homes featuring 14 guest rooms, serving full, hot breakfasts.

127 Jefferson Court
West Newton, PA 15089
724.872.0792
brightmorningbb.com

The Ruins Project at Sager Mosaics

Tour a giant mosaic museum that tells the stories of coal. Mosaic art and hand-crafted jewelry. Artisan-made GAP gifts. Leona's famous ice cream sandwiches.

Mile marker 104 in Whitsett
rachel@sagermosaics.com
www.sagermosaics.com to book
your Ruins Tour reservations

The Historic
PLUMER
GUEST HOUSE
Circa 1814

Plumer Guest House

Perfect for cyclists & outdoor enthusiasts. Clean, comfortable with a common area kitchen & living rm. Grab & go breakfast. Single rooms or entire house is available, 12 guest max, 3 bedrooms, 6 beds, & 2 baths.

131 S. Water, West Newton, Pa 15089
Mile 114, .025 mile off the trail
Book your stay on Airbnb:
abnb.me/9zwNqeKy04
or call Greg direct 412-482-7066

McKeesport's 258-acre Renziehausen Park Rose Garden and Arboretum contains some 1,800 rose bushes in 28 beds, and is worth a bit of road riding for a picnic lunch.

Photo: Great Allegheny Passage Conservancy

McKEESPORT

ALLEGHENY COUNTY, PENNSYLVANIA

ELEVATION 752 FEET • GAP 132.5

Located at the confluence of the Youghiogheny and Monongahela Rivers, McKeesport was, for over a hundred years, the headquarters for **National Tube Works**, the country's preeminent manufacturer of steel tubes, pipes, poles, and scores of similar items that undergirded the American industrial revolution. During World War II, the city's factories employed more than 10,000 people making war materiel and vital defense supplies. Today, National Tube Works is closed, but you can still see modern pipe and tube manufacturers using its renovated facilities.

Next to the GAP, the **McKeesport Marina** accommodates more than 200 watercraft, and sports a picnic pavilion and fishing pier. Nearby are some retail shops and casual eateries.

The city's **Renziehausen Park** features a 400-square-foot perennial garden, beds that contain over 1,800 roses, a pond, and a butterfly garden. The park also hosts the **International Village**, McKeesport's annual heritage festival which celebrates nationalities around the world, especially those with deep roots in the immigrant-rich Mon Valley.

Worth a visit is the **McKeesport Regional History and Heritage Center**, featuring exhibits preserving the stories, photos, and artifacts critical to the Mon Valley's industrial heritage. The museum proudly houses the very first schoolhouse to be erected in McKeesport in 1832. Additionally, the **Carnegie Library of McKeesport**, designed by noted Pittsburgh architect William J. East and opened in 1902, is a local treasure.

Because of McKeesport's built environment, the GAP follows a quiet on-street route for about a half-mile. From near the fire station, you can access the "Clairton Connector," a five-mile on-road route that meets the popular **Montour Trail** (see map on page 86.)

VISITOR INFORMATION

| 11 | McKeesport City Hall | 675-5020 |

FOOD AND DRINK

38	Big Shot Bob's	872-4410
2	Broadway Pizza	673-6928
39	Café Hibiscus	
29	Cal's Cantina	751-9070
43	Christy Park Cones	780-4303
7	Dunkin Donuts	872-4494
14	Eat 'n Park	664-9148
27	The Elbow Room	672-7900
25	Fonzi's East End Grill	664-5943
40	Guilty Pleasure Nutrition	664-7005
41	Hi Eatery	398-9708
30	Hoot's Again	664-4668
26	Kings Fried Chicken	896-4764
23	Lampert's Market – Fine Meats & Deli	664-7371
4	McKees Point Café	678-6979
24	McKeesport Fish & Chicken	896-6766
31	Mellon's Pub	751-3285
17	Minerva Bakery	673-2863
18	Pazzo Italian Grill	678-8189
32	Pizza & Gyro Express	672-2182
33	Pizza Burgh	678-2112
34	Puzzlers Restaurant and Lounge	672-2111
36	The Roo Bar	259-3766
42	Scotty's Ice Cream Delights	664-4364
35	Sloppy Dogs	872-5466
10	Subway	678-7640
37	Tillie's Restaurant	672-7557
28	Tony's Restaurant	733-8179

PARKS AND ATTRACTIONS

21	Carnegie Library of McKeesport	672-0625
6	J.F.K. Memorial Park	
22	McKeesport Little Theater	673-1100
19	McKeesport Regional History and Heritage Center	678-1832
4	Marina at McKees Point	678-6979
3	The Palisades	896-1995
20	Renziehausen Park and Rose Garden	563-6755
20	Rose Garden operated by The Garden Club of McKeesport	751-7777

EMERGENCIES AND PUBLIC SERVICES

| 5 | McKeesport Police Station | 675-5015 |
| 1 | United States Postal Service | 672-9722 |

SHOPS AND OTHER SERVICES

8	CVS	678-6769
15	Dollar General	677-0450
13	Rite Aid	672-3853
16	Shop 'n Save	672-7820

BANKING AND ATM'S

| 9 | Dollar Bank | 673-7366 |
| 12 | PNC Bank | 678-6125 |

All phone numbers are preceded by (412) unless otherwise noted

McKEESPORT

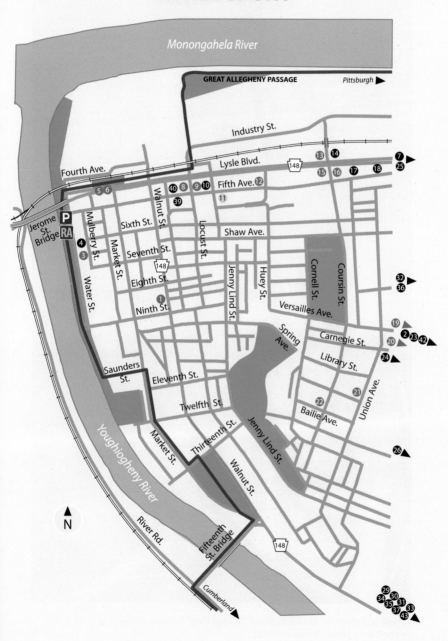

P indicates Trailhead Parking   RA indicates River Access

A new sculpture by Jim West titled "Yellow Dog" honors steelworkers, adjacent to the Pump House in Homestead.

Photo: Rivers of Steel National Heritage Area

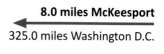

8.0 miles McKeesport

325.0 miles Washington D.C.

South Side 4.7 miles

Pittsburgh 8.3 miles

MUNHALL, WEST HOMESTEAD, AND

HOMESTEAD

ALLEGHENY COUNTY, PENNSYLVANIA

ELEVATION 750 FEET • GAP 140.5

The contiguous communities of Munhall, Homestead, and West Homestead were built on the steelmaking and machining industries, the best known of which was the **Homestead Steel Works**, a sprawling campus of manufacturing might that was fed by the region's coal resources and bolstered by extensive railroad and river access. Scaled up by **U.S. Steel** for most of the 20th century, largely on the backs of immigrant laborers and their descendants, it employed nearly 15,000 people during World War II. The 1892 **Homestead Lockout and Strike** – during the ownership of Andrew Carnegie – was among the first deadly management-labor disputes in American history, and ended only after Carnegie deployed armed guards and called in state militia.

In Homestead sits the **Bost Building**, the union headquarters throughout the strike, and now the visitor center for the **Rivers of Steel National Heritage Area**. Explore the exhibit space, or take a self-guided historical tour of the borough with one of their portable DVD players. Local restaurants, craft breweries, and bakeries dot the **Eighth Avenue Historic District**. The **Carnegie Library of Homestead**, in Munhall, built in 1896 and later endowed by Carnegie himself, is in the French Renaissance style and is located a few blocks away.

A section of the GAP in Munhall uses dedicated bike lanes to skirt a riverside manufacturing plant, and then passes by the **Pump House**, one of the Homestead Steel Works' remaining buildings, well-worth a stop for a tour of its exhibits. Or pause at the adjacent labyrinth created by artist Lorraine Vullo as a place of reflection and remembrance. Today, **The Waterfront's** restaurants and retailers span all three boroughs, and travelers can find hotels, grocers, and entertainment en route.

Steel Valley Bike Oasis 🚲

The towns of *Homestead, West Homestead* and *Munhall*, nestled along the Monongahela River, continue to reflect the spirit that made the area a capital of industry a century ago. This is evident in the shopping and entertainment of the Waterfront, whose arrival in 1999 ushered in a new era. Beyond the energy of the Waterfront await architectural gems, historic landmarks, Kennywood Amusement Park, Sandcastle Waterpark and cultural treasures in the Avenues of the Steel Valley.

Attractions

1   Steel Heritage History Center 412.464.4020
2   Pump House
3   Homestead Labyrinth
4   Stacks
5   Bald Eagles Nest
6   Great Allegheny Passage (Bike Trail)
8   Enix Brewing Bowling 412.656.2107
9   Community Garden 7th & Amity
10 Carnegie Library & Music Hall 412.462.3444
11 AMC Loews Theatre 412.462.6550
12 Improv Comedy Club 412.462.5233
13 Bulgarian Macedonian National
     Education & Cultural Center 412.461.6188
14 Kennywood Amusement Park 412.461.0500
15 Sandcastle Water Park 412.462.6666
16 Local Motion Yoga and Spinning 412.407.7863
68 Escape Room 412.742.4645
69 Dragon's Den
81 Ace Axe Throwing 412.368.8579

Banks

18 First Commonwealth 412.886.2501
19 PNC 412.461.8512
20 Citizens 412.462.8455
21 Tri-Boro Credit Union 412.461.3018
22 First National 412.368.3157

Bikes

23 Bike Fix Station
24 Dick's Sporting Goods 412.476.9940
25 Target 412.464.2522

← 7 miles to Pittsburgh

Funded by Steel Valley Enterprise Zone Corp.

← 15
← 5

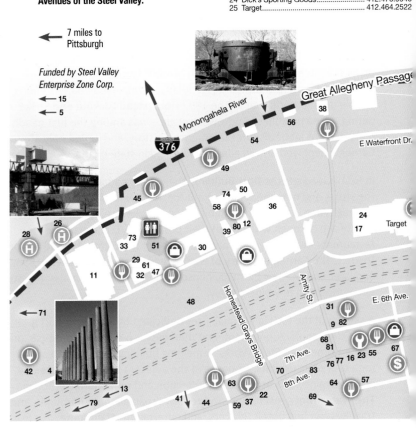

Monongahela River

Great Allegheny Passage

376

E Waterfront Dr.

Target

Amity St.

Homestead Grays Bridge

E. 6th Ave.

7th Ave.

8th Ave.

Hotels

26 Hampton Inn & Suites 412.462.4226
27 Holiday Inn Express 412.205.3904
28 Courtyard Marriott............................. 412.462.7301

Food & Drink

11 AMC Loews Theatre 412.462.6550
17 Wine and Spirits................................ 412.464.2574
29 Bar Louie 412.462.6400
30 Barnes & Noble 412.462.5743
31 Blue Dust 412.461.6220
32 Bravo Cucina Italiana 412.461.1444
33 Burgatory.. 412.461.2200
34 Chick-fil-A 412.462.9202
35 Conrad's... 412.462.3534
36 Dave & Busters 412.462.1500
37 Duke's Upper Deck 412.461.8124
38 Eat'n Park... 412.464.7275
39 Primanti Bros.................................... 412.461.1469
40 Pido Pub... 412.461.9540
41 KFC 412.461.7058
42 Longhorn Steakhouse........................ 412.476.8195
43 McDonald's 412.461.1002
44 Me Lyng.. 412.464.1477
45 Mitchell's Fish Market 412.476.8844
46 Old School Italian Sandwich Shop..... 412.205.3866
47 Panera Bread 412.464.1244
48 PF Chang's China Bistro.................... 412.464.0640
49 Red Robin 412.461.2044
50 Rock Bottom Brewery........................ 412.462.2739
51 Starbucks.. 412.461.2500
52 Steak 'n Shake.................................. 412.461.6545

53 Primanti Bros.................................... 412.461.1469
54 TGI Friday's 412.462.8443
55 Honest John's 412.205.3448
56 Uno Chicago Grill............................... 412.462.8667
57 Voodoo Brewery Homestead.............. 412.368.8973
58 Yokoso.. 412.461.8800
59 Eighth & Hays................................... 412.326.0009
61 Jimmy John's 412.461.1290
62 Wendy's.. 412.462.0860
63 Subway 412.464.9074
64 Capri Pizza 412.461.1203
65 Disallo's Pizza................................... 412.462.5070
66 Mama Pepinos................................... 412.464.2200
67 Dorothy Six Café 412.464.9023
72 8th Avenue Café 412.368.8218
73 Rocket Fizz 412.461.6462
74 Sing Sing.. 412.461.7426
76 RB Winery Homestead 412.789.8272
77 Steel Valley Roasters 412.532.8484
82 The Forge Wine Bar 202.805.0918
83 Live Fresh... 412.530.2640

Bakeries

78 Mantsch Blue Bonnett Bakery........... 412.462.4957
79 Nancy B Bakery 412.462.6222
80 Cakery Square 412.514.9443

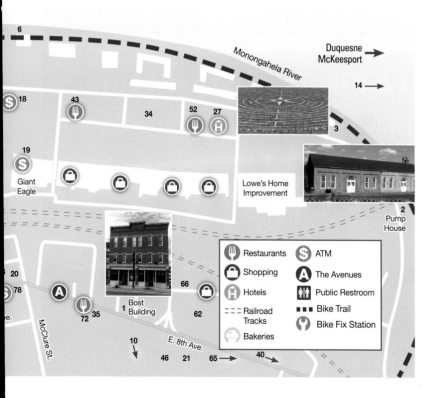

COURTYARD
BY MARRIOTT
PITTSBURGH WATERFRONT

Courtyard by Marriott

Bike the GAP and start at the Courtyard. Located on GAP trail mile-marker 141.
Bike storage options available. Accommodates large groups.

Request GAP rate: 412-462-7301 or visit marriott.com/pithw and enter Corporate Promo Code GP8
401 West Waterfront Drive
W Homestead, PA 15120

PRIMANTI BROS.

Primanti Bros.

We'll always be who we've always been – fresh, house-made ingredients, big sandwiches and awesome deals on the coldest drinks, including half-price happy hour.
So pull up a barstool, order a drink or a sandwich and settle in. Visit us at:

The Waterfront
152 East Bridge St., Homestead
& Market Square
2 South Market Square, Pittsburgh

Borough of West Homestead

West Homestead Borough

Pride in our heritage, confidence in our future. Rest and refresh body and spirit at the amenities available in our town, just a short ride from the GAP trail. Come visit us!

456 West 8th Avenue
www.westhomesteadpa.com
Find us on Facebook
and twitter @WestHomestead

ROCK·BOTTOM
RESTAURANT & BREWERY

Rock Bottom Restaurant & Brewery

Get amazing food, featuring burgers, flatbreads, salads, vegetarian options, and unique craft beer at Rock Bottom Restaurant & Brewery in Homestead at the Waterfront Mile 141. Open daily from 11am – 11pm.

171 E Bridge St. Homestead, PA
412-685-6010
www.rockbottom.com

This mural by Monica Cervone McElwain, visible along East Carson Street, celebrates Pittsburgh's South Side.

Photo: Great Allegheny Passage Conservancy

PITTSBURGH'S

SOUTH SIDE

ALLEGHENY COUNTY, PENNSYLVANIA

ELEVATION 741 FEET • GAP 145.2

Pittsburgh's South Side was founded as a separate city, Birmingham, and was first known as the locus of America's glassmaking industry – the Ripley Glass Company building still stands on Bingham Street – before becoming the headquarters for **Jones and Laughlin Steel Company** and then even better associated with metal foundries and steel mills. Annexed by Pittsburgh in 1872, the South Side retains outsized commercial structures like the neo-classical **Iron and Glass Bank Building** and the **Duquesne Brewery Clock** – still marking time with its one-ton minute hand.

Today, Pittsburgh's South Side contains the city's core social scene, particularly for college students, with coffee shops, restaurants, shot-and-a-beer pubs, theaters, retailers, art and photo galleries, clothiers, bookstores, and a significant nightlife. **East Carson Street** is a nationally designated Historic District, and for 13 blocks, three- and four-story Romanesque, Italianate, and Second Empire storefronts welcome customers and tourists. Bike-friendly businesses abound.

Two remaining funicular railways – the **Duquesne Incline** and **Monongahela Incline** – take you up to the city's best views from the Mt. Washington neighborhood. Alternatively, you can wander the South Side's residential slopes using any of the 68 sets of public stairs. Halfway up the slopes are the gardens and grounds of the 1859 **St. Paul of the Cross Monastery**, a quiet spot for reflection, or for viewing the South Side business district and downtown skyline.

As it approaches the South Side, the GAP runs between the Monongahela River and the Pittsburgh Steelers' training facility along Water Street, before turning right over the **Hot Metal Bridge**.

Check out what's happening at **www.southsidechamber.org**.

WELCOME TO SOUTH SIDE ☎ 412-

1. South Side Chamber of Commerce southsidechamber.org	431-3360

LODGING

2. Sheraton PGH Station Sq	261-2000
3. South Side Travelers Rest	623-9343
4. Holiday Inn Express	488-1130
5. Hotel Indigo	621-0880
6. Hyatt House PGH-SSW	390-2477
7. SpringHill Suites PGH-SSW	488-8003

FOOD & DRINK

8. Cilantro & Ajo	432-5708
9. Café du Jour	488-9695
10. Jack's	431-3644
11. Streets on Carson	918-1006
12. Kassab's Lebanese	381-1820
13. The Urban Tap	586-7499
14. 12 Whiskey BBQ+Meatballs	742-4024
15. Doce Taqueria	238-8518
16. Vault Taproom+Piggy Bank	904-4462
17. Smiling Moose	431-4668
18. Big Shot Bobs	381-7468
19. Starbucks	381-7183
20. O'Leary's Diner	431-8100
21. Carson City Saloon	381-3202
22. Le Bodega Taqueria	586-4596
23. Fudge Farm	315-7893
24. OddBalls	235-7566
25. Carson Street Deli & Beer	381-3335
26. Local Bar + Kitchen	904-3993
27. Swirl Penguins Ice Cream	504-1850
28. Mario's Saloon-South Side	381-5610
29. Nakama Japanese Steak	381-6000
30. South Side BBQ Company	381-4566
31. Dish Osteria & Bar	390-2012
32. Cambod-ican Kitchen	381-6199
33. Street Noodles	488-8888
34. Milk Shake Factory	488-1808
35. Tres Rios Mexican Kitchen	930-0868
36. Delanie's Coffee	536-8778
37. Bruegger's Bagels	381-2833
38. Fat Head's Saloon	431-7433
39. Carmi Soul Food	231-0100
40. Pub Chip Shop	381-2247
41. Piper's Pub	381-3977
42. Doughbar Pizzeria	910-9100
43. Primanti Bros.	381-2583
44. Benny Fierro's Pizza	709-6077
45. Carmella's Plates & Pints	918-1215
46. Hello Bistro	390-1922
47. Smokin' Joe's Saloon	431-6757
48. Tiki Lounge	381-8454
49. The Colombian Spot	381-9000
50. Mad Noodles	251-0558
51. Churn Ice Cream & Coffee	431-3058
52. Cancilla's Sicilian Pizzeria	481-9337
53. Le Petit Cafe & Grille	775-3653
54. Lins Asian Fusion	251-0228
55. Bonfire Food & Drink	481-3473
56. Stagioni	586-4738
57. Acacia	488-1800
58. Dive Bar	481-2969
59. The Library	381-0517
60. LaPalapa Mexican Kitchen	586-7015
61. Thai Me Up	488-8893
62. Cupka's Café 2	431-9691
63. The Pretzel Shop	431-2574
64. 23rd & Vine	235-7447
65. Double Wide Grill	390-1111
66. OTB Bicycle Cafe	381-3698
67. The Zenith	481-4833
68. Cup Ka Joe	390-1563
69. Big Dog Coffee	586-7306
70. Hofbrauhaus PGH	224-2328
71. Nadine's Restaurant	481-1793
72. Waffles INCaffeinated	301-1763

ATTRACTIONS

73. Pittsburgh Riverhounds	224-4900
74. Station Square	800-859-8959
75. Victory Pointe Gaming	251-5150
76. Club Cafe	431-4950
77. City Theatre	431-4400
78. Foxtail	651-4713
79. Rex Theater	667-2900
80. Jimmy D's NightSpot	431-5095
81. ASCEND Pittsburgh	745-2141
82. Carnegie Library	431-0505
83. Southside Works	710-7220

SHOPS & RETAIL

84. Salvation Army Store	481-7900
85. Cindy Esser's Floral Shop	431-6188
86. Buffalo Exchange	431-5389
87. NOLAC	533-3434
88. Slacker	381-3911
89. Pittsburgh Guitars	431-0700
90. Copies at Carson	481-4875
91. Illegal Apparel	784-6531
92. Fig Leaf Boutique	431-7700
93. Ethik Worldwide	390-3788
94. The Culture Shop	481-8284
95. Three Rivers Vintage	431-2140
96. UPS Store	381-7755
97. Sittoy Boutique	607-699-9396
98. Viral on Carson	709-6998
99. Nick's Imports	512-0346
100. Ablyn Fashions	431-1101
101. Highway Robbery Vintage	251-0818
102. Lucy's Clothing Shop	347-806-8194
103. S&S Candy and Cigar	481-6577
104. Premium Wine & Spirits	431-0439
105. Buddy's Brews on Carson	709-6353
106. Hometowne Sports	471-7280
107. Goodwill Store	481-5390
108. Vapor Galleria	481-8273

BIKE & TRAIL

109. Krazy Scooter	944-9066
110. THICK Bikes	390-3590
111. REI	488-9410

BANKING & ATM

112. Riverset Credit Union	488-2525
113. First National Bank	432-5705
114. Dollar Bank	431-4157
115. PNC Bank	431-2581
116. Farmers National Bank	431-9191
117. Citizens Bank-Giant Eagle	431-8209
118. Citizens Bank	431-0200

SALONS & BARBER SHOPS

119. J's Master Barbers	728-8052
120. Great Clips	251-0548
121. Phillip Pelusi	488-6618
122. Cost Cutters	431-4545

ESSENTIALS

123. Coen Markets S 10th St	293-1014
124. Vogt Hardware	488-4399
125. MetroPCS	904-3984
126. Rite Aid Pharmacy	481-8818
127. Giant Eagle Supermarket	488-1816
128. Family Dollar	995-2599
129. T Mobile	489-0671
130. Dirty Franky's Laundromat	759-5723
131. Coen Markets S 24th St	431-3550
132. GetGo Cafe + Market	481-6430

WELLNESS

133. Five Star Dentistry	381-3373
134. Ploucha Chiropractic	381-4422
135. Pusz & Siegel Eyecare	381-1542
136. City Vets	483-1700
137. UPMC Mercy Outpatient	488-5550
138. Quick Drip IV	223-5393

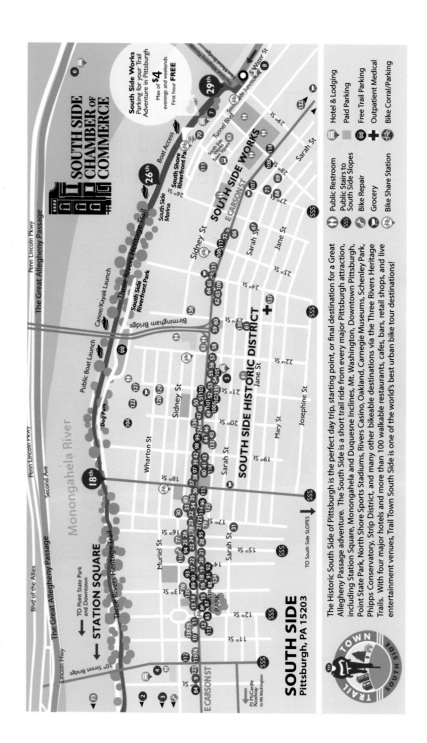

The Historic South Side of Pittsburgh is the perfect day trip, starting point, or final destination for a Great Allegheny Passage adventure. The South Side is a short trail ride from every major Pittsburgh attraction, including Station Square, Monongahela and Duquesne Inclines, Mt. Washington, Downtown Pittsburgh, Point State Park, North Shore Sports Stadiums, Rivers Casino, Oakland, Carnegie Museums, Schenley Park, Phipps Conservatory, Strip District, and many other bikeable destinations via the Three Rivers Heritage Trails. With four major hotels and more than 100 walkable restaurants, cafes, bars, retail shops, and live entertainment venues, Trail Town South Side is one of the world's best urban bike tour destinations!

Redbud along the Allegheny River, looking toward the Andy Warhol Bridge into Downtown Pittsburgh.

Photo: Katherine Sikma

DOWNTOWN

PITTSBURGH

ALLEGHENY COUNTY, PENNSYLVANIA

ELEVATION 712 FEET • GAP 148.8

Once renowned as the world center for steel production and related manufacturing, Pittsburgh is now a hub for medical research, higher education, tech startups, and unique treasures like the **Andy Warhol Museum** and **August Wilson African American Cultural Center**. It's home to 446 bridges (more than any city in the world!), scores of hilly neighborhoods, dozens of craft beer breweries, three famous sports teams, and a burgeoning bicycling community. It's a city proud of its working-class roots, and a wonderful endpoint on your journey west.

Once over the **Hot Metal Bridge**, the GAP follows the Eliza Furnace Trail – named for a series of Jones and Laughlin blast furnaces that occupied the banks of the Monongahela for over 100 years – all the way downtown. Cross Grant Street, and ride a dedicated bike/pedestrian chute to Smithfield Street. To your left is the **Smithfield Street Bridge**, an 1883 lenticular truss bridge named a National Historic Civic Engineering Landmark, and across it, the historic **Pittsburgh and Lake Erie Railroad** terminal, which now houses the Grand Concourse Hotel.

Follow the bike/ped switchback down to the **Monongahela Wharf Landing** and ride into **Point State Park** to find the western terminus of the GAP where the Monogahela and Allegheny Rivers meet. (There's an on-street alternative if need be – see page 222). Stop in at the **Fort Pitt Museum** to learn about Pittsburgh's pivotal role during the French and Indian War. Gather at the park's famous fountain to take in the entire downtown cityscape. Nearby **Market Square** contains restaurants, farmers' markets, and live entertainment. Ride the Penn Avenue bike lanes to access the **Amtrak** station, or head to the **Strip District** for fresh produce, art galleries, and quirky cafes.

For ideas and events, go to **www.visitpittsburgh.com**.

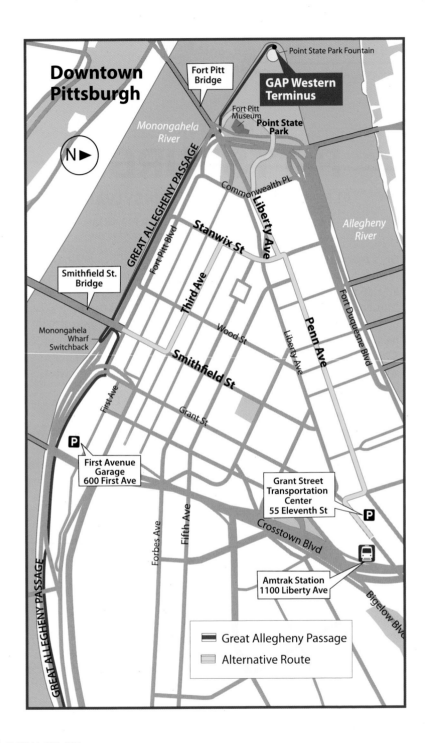

Downtown Pittsburgh

Point State Park Fountain

Fort Pitt Bridge

GAP Western Terminus

Fort Pitt Museum

Monongahela River

Point State Park

Commonwealth Pl

Allegheny River

GREAT ALLEGHENY PASSAGE

Stanwix St

Liberty Ave

Fort Pitt Blvd

Third Ave

Smithfield St. Bridge

Wood St

Penn Ave

Fort Duquesne Blvd

Monongahela Wharf Switchback

Smithfield St

Liberty Ave

First Ave

Grant St

P First Avenue Garage 600 First Ave

Grant Street Transportation Center 55 Eleventh St P

Forbes Ave

Fifth Ave

Crosstown Blvd

Amtrak Station 1100 Liberty Ave

Bigelow Blvd

GREAT ALLEGHENY PASSAGE

Great Allegheny Passage

Alternative Route

NAVIGATING DOWNTOWN PITTSBURGH

The GAP's western terminus is at the tip of Point State Park in Downtown Pittsburgh. If you're riding from Cumberland into Pittsburgh, make your way to the end of the marked path at Grant Street. Cross Grant Street and ride on a dedicated bike/ped chute to Smithfield Street. Turn left and descend the new Monongahela Wharf Switchback. Ride the flat promenade along the river, and up a ramp into the back of Point State Park, behind the state park office building. This is the official route, entirely off city streets, and is marked in red on the map to the left.

If the wharf is closed due to high water (about 45 days a year), do not go down the switchback. Instead, take a 0.75 mile on-street alternative marked on the pavement with sharrows and bike lanes. Turn right on Smithfield Street, left on Third Avenue, right on Stanwix Street, left on Penn Avenue (it will turn into Liberty Avenue), and into Point State Park. See this alternative route, marked in yellow, on the map to the left. If you're not comfortable riding this alternative route, please walk your bike on the sidewalks that parallel it. After entering Point State Park, ride over the portal bridge and make your way past the Fort Pitt Museum, to the park's iconic fountain and a bronze medallion marking the GAP's end.

If you are starting your journey inside Point State Park and are headed to Cumberland, ride from the bronze medallion along the Monongahela River and then up behind the state park office building. Follow a narrow corridor and ramp down to the Monongahela Wharf. Ride the promenade along the river, and go up the new Monongahela Wharf Switchback. Make a hard right onto a bike/ped chute. Cross Grant Street and you're on your way. This is the official route, marked in red on the map to the left.

If the wharf is closed due to high water (about 45 days a year), do not go behind the state park office. Instead, proceed to the park's

Photo: Ziaur Rahman

main exit and follow a 0.75 mile on-route alternative route that uses bike lanes and sharrows, starting with Liberty Avenue (which turns into Penn Avenue). Turn right on Stanwix, left onto Third Avenue, and right onto Smithfield Street. Instead of crossing the Smithfield Street Bridge, turn left on a bike/ped chute. Cross Grant Street and you're on your way. See this alternative route, marked in yellow, on the map to the left.

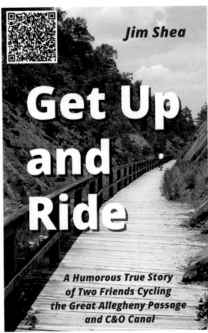

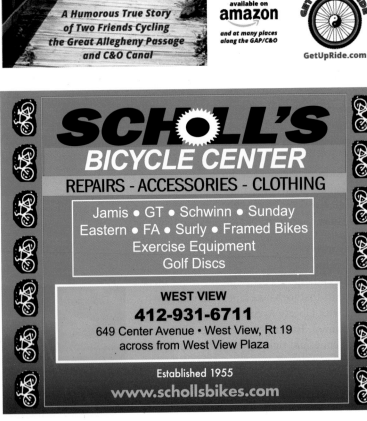

Adam Solar Rides

We rent fully outfitted electric bikes for your GAP and C&O adventure! Pittsburgh's original eBike shop with over 100 eBikes in stock! Tues-Fri 10-6. Sat 10-4. Mon by Apt.

1912 Mayview Road
Bridgeville PA 15017
412-220-1900 shop
412-495-6374 cell/txt
ASR@AdamSolarRides.com

Traveler's Rest Hotel

Independent hotel located 1.7 miles from start of the GAP. Private rooms, indoor bike and gear storage, tuning and wash station, and communal kitchen.

27 South 6th St
Pittsburgh, PA 15203
info@SSTRpgh.com
(412) 623-9343
SSTRpgh.com
@SSTRpgh | fb.com/SSTRpgh

Bear Dog Bicycles

Full service sales and repairs. Our team can fix your favorite ride or help you find a new one. In Historic Northside. Easy access to the Riverfront and GAP trails.

857 Dounton Way
Pittsburgh 15233
412-231-1790
www.beardogbikes.com
@beardogbicycles

Bill's Car Service & Transport

A private transportation company serving the GAP and C&O Trails, and Pittsburgh International Airport. Shuttle service, luggage and bicycle transport. 24 hours a day, 7 days a week.

412-855-4484
billscarservice.com
billscarservice@gmail.com

SUPPORT THE TRAILKEEPERS

The **Great Allegheny Passage** was built and is stewarded by a variety of local organizations, working cooperatively in conjunction with the nonprofit **Great Allegheny Passage Conservancy**. It takes tens of thousands of hours each year to keep the GAP fit for service. Hundreds of faithful, long-serving volunteers handle the lion's share of these year-round efforts, which includes cutting grass, removing fallen trees, supplying firewood, water, and clean shelters at some campgrounds, digging out from landslides, resurfacing trail sections, installing fences, cutting back invasive weed, clearing culverts under the trail surface, picking up trash left by travelers, clearing fallen rocks, fixing bollards, and painting over graffiti. They also recruit and coordinate major efforts to deal with emergency repairs and enhancements funded in part by proceeds from *TrailGuide*.

Support the following affiliated groups directly by volunteering or giving:

- Allegany County, Md. and **Mountain Maryland Trails**
- Somerset County, Pa. and the **Somerset County Recreation and Trails Association**
- Ohiopyle State Park and **Friends of Ohiopyle**
- Regional Trail Corporation and the **Yough River Trail Council, Whitsett-Fayette Yough Trail Chapter, Westmoreland Yough Trail Chapter, Mon/Yough Trail Council, McKeesport Trail Commission, and Steel Valley Trail Council**, with help from the **Westmoreland County Parks Department**
- City of Pittsburgh and **Friends of the Riverfront**
- Point State Park

The Great Allegheny Passage Conservancy also coordinates infrared and manual trail counts along the Great Allegheny Passage, works with municipalities to update wayfinding signage, draws media attention to the Washington, D.C. to Pittsburgh journey, and promotes the GAP to new audiences around the country. Make a tax-deductible donation at www.gaptrail.org.

The **Chesapeake & Ohio Canal National Historical Park**, a gem of the National Park System, manages the **C&O Canal Towpath**. The **C&O Canal Trust** is its official nonprofit partner and works in partnership with the National Park Service to protect, restore, and promote the C&O Canal and Towpath, and operates the Canal Quarters program. Support the C&O Canal Trust at www.canaltrust.org.

BACK LOCAL BUSINESSES

Most of your journey along the C&O Canal Towpath and Great Allegheny Passage takes you through rural areas far from the Washington, D.C. and Pittsburgh metropolitan areas. Our canal towns and trail towns, once known for coal, lumber, coke, paper, or farming, have pivoted to become hospitable stops for travelers. Their presence differentiates this journey from other long-distance hiking and bicycling adventures, where services are scarce. Yet most businesses are run by folks who work long hours and put in a lot of sweat equity. Their margins are thin. They help one another in down times, and celebrate together when the "trail economy" brings a bit of flourishing to town. They're often creative, always industrious, and provide great service for modest prices.

Proprietors of Donges Drive-In and Motel, Meyersdale.

Photo: Anita Harnish

Many business owners advertise here in *TrailGuide*, knowing that a portion of its proceeds funds emergency repairs and enhancements performed largely by volunteers along the C&O Canal Towpath and Great Allegheny Passage. Choose your lodging, meals, and services from among these generous folks as you plan your next overnight or thru-trip!

ALPHABETICAL INDEX TO ADVERTISERS

Note on locations: Many services are in the town's business district, although some may be several miles away. Please refer to their advertisements for location and contact information.

LODGING

See camping options on index page 232 and 38-39.

FOOD & BEVERAGE

TOUR OPERATORS / SHUTTLE SERVICES

BICYCLE RENTAL / SALES / SERVICE

Brunswick, Md.
  Three Points Cycle, 117
Knoxville, Md.
  River & Trail Outfitters, 122
Shepherdstown, W.Va.
  Shepherdstown Pedal and Paddle, 129
Hancock, Md.
  C&O Bicycle & Bunkhouse, 140
Cumberland, Md.
  Wheelzup Adventures & Shuttles, 149
Frostburg, Md.
  Allegheny Trail House B&B, 157
Confluence, Pa.
  Allegheny Recumbent Tours, 178
  Confluence Cyclery, 178
Ohiopyle, Pa.
  Ohiopyle Suites, 187
  Wilderness Voyageurs, 186

Uniontown, Pa.
  Jolt Bike, Inside Front Cover
Connellsville, Pa.
  Bikes Unlimited, 195
  Comfort Inn, 194
West Newton, Pa.
  2 Wheel Escapes, 32
  West Newton Bicycle Shop, 200
Pittsburgh's South Side
  Thick Bikes, 219
Downtown Pittsburgh
  Bear Dog Bicycles, 225
  Golden Triangle Bike, 24
  Noble Invention Bike Touring, 24
West View, Pa.
  Scholl's Bicycle Center, 224
Bridgeville, Pa.
  Adam Solar Rides, 225

CAMPING

Bethesda, Md.
  C&O Canal Quarters (seven lockhouses), 62
Meyersdale, Pa.
  PA Maple Festival Campground, 167
Adelaide, Pa.
  Uniontown KOA, 193

Belle Vernon, Pa.
  Cedar Creek Park, 202
West Newton, Pa.
  GAP Trail Campground, 201

EXPERIENCES

Washington, D.C.
  DC Bicycling Concierge, 32
Brunswick, Md.
  Brunswick Heritage Museum, 115
Frostburg, Md.
  Tracks & Yaks, 68
Ohiopyle, Pa.
  Fallingwater, 28

Ohiopyle, Pa.
  Kentuck Knob, 28
Whitsett, Pa.
  Sager Mosaics and The Ruins Project, 203
Homestead, Pa.
  Rivers of Steel Heritage Corporation, 212

SPIRITS

Brunswick, Md.
  Smoketown Brewing Station, 117
Shepherdstown, W.Va.
  Bavarian Inn Resort & Brewing Company, 128
Frostburg, Md.
  Route 40 Brewing & Distilling Company, 156
  Toasted Goat Craft Winery & Restaurant, 156

Rockwood, Pa.
  Trailhead Brewing Company, 173
Homestead, Pa.
  Rock Bottom Restaurant & Brewery, 213